THE FOILING DINGHY BOOK

DINGHY FOILING FROM START TO FINISH

To my parents David and Margaret who supported my passion for sailing, and to Paloma, Natalia and Naomi for showing me the things that are more important than sailing.

THE FOILING DINGHY BOOK
DINGHY FOILING FROM **START TO FINISH**

Alan Hillman

FERNHURST
BOOKS

First published in 2018 by Fernhurst Books Limited

The Windmill, Mill Lane, Harbury, Leamington Spa, Warwickshire. CV33 9HP. UK
Tel: +44 (0) 1926 337488 | www.fernhurstbooks.com

A catalogue record for this book is available from the British Library
ISBN 978-1-912177-04-2

The author and publisher would like to express their considerable thanks to Richard Langdon for taking most of the Moth photographs.

Front cover and most Moth photographs © Richard Langdon, Ocean Images

All F101 and most Waszp photographs and p9, 13 (top), 17 (right), 22 (top), 25, 32, 33, 35 (right), 36, 37 (top), 73, 74, 83, 96 © Alan Hillman / David Hillman / Geoff Cox / Foiling World / Pro-Vela

p8: Gerald New; back cover (middle), 18 (bottom), 20 (bottom), 26, 29, 79, 93: Martina Orsini © Foiling Week; p12 (left): Tom Gruitt; p12 (right): Tim Hore; p15, 16: James Grogono; p17 (top left): Andy Patterson; p17 (middle left): Brett Burvill; p17 (bottom left): John Illet; p18 (top), 31: Walter Cooper; p19 (top): Onefly; p20 (top left): Wildwind; p20 (top right): Nichola Strehle / Walti Gauer; p34, 35 (bottom left): Jeremy Atkins; p44: Werner Scheidegger; p106: Glide Free Design

Designed & typeset by Rachel Atkins
Illustrated by Maggie Nelson
Printed in the UK by Latimer Trend

ALAN HILLMAN

FOILING MOTH SAILOR & INSTRUCTOR, F101 CREATOR

Alan Hillman's lifetime in the sailing world has seen him experience many aspects of the sport, particularly in the area of coaching in which he has over 30 years' experience. His extensive CV includes:

- RYA Windsurfing Manager, where he developed their training programmes and overseas centres
- Setting up the high performance sailing and windsurfing centre Team Unlimited in Spain with Rob Andrews
- Race Directing for the Extreme 40s and the Barcelona World Race
- Establishing Pro-Vela in Spain, offering personalised coaching, particularly in foiling Moths
- Owning Sportsboat World (distributors of the SB20) and, more recently, Foiling World (creators of the F101) with Jerry Hill and Rob Andrews

One of his greatest strengths is his ability to analyse sailing manoeuvres, break them down into their constituent parts and then teach sailors those elements in a memorable way.

As a competitor, Alan has won National schools titles in both sailing and windsurfing through to senior National titles in the Laser 4000 and SB20 classes.

Alan learnt to sail a foiling International Moth the hard way – by teaching himself: involving many hours on, in and under the water. He has distilled this experience into the programme offered at Pro-Vela where he has introduced many sailors to foiling, including:

- Sir Ben Ainslie
- Ian Walker
- Mike Golding
- Andreas John

This experience is now made more widely available through this book.

Alan Hillman at Pro-Vela in Murcia, Spain

CONTENTS

Mike Lennon sailing his Thinnair design

FOREWORD
BY MIKE LENNON

Looking at the entry list for the 2017 International Moth World Championships shows what many of the world's top sailors do for fun — they sail foiling dinghies! The entry list was like a Who's Who of America's Cup and Olympic sailors.

Sailing a foiling Moth is not only fun, it is also quite a challenge to learn how to do it and this book provides a perfect manual. Alan Hillman has been coaching people to sail International Moths for many years and is just the right person to introduce you to this.

But where the International Moth leads, others follow, and so now there are designs which make foiling more accessible to the average sailor. Foiling such craft still has its challenges and you still need to learn how to do it and get the most out of it. Again, this book provides you with that knowledge.

So, whether you are just interested in the idea of foiling dinghies, you want to learn how to foil in one of the modern designs or you want to go the full hog and learn how to sail a foiling Moth, this is the book for you. Packed full of expert advice, top tips and with over 300 photographs, it explains clearly how to foil.

Foiling is here to stay and will only grow and grow. With this book you will be able to understand what foiling is and how you can join in.

I look forward to seeing you flying above the water soon!

Mike Lennon
Past International Moth UK & European Champion
Past International 14, Melges 24 & Scorpion UK National Champion
Moth designer, sailmaker & sailing clothing manufacturer

PART 1
BACKGROUND

INTRODUCTION

Overview: This book will set out the basic skills and techniques that are required when learning to sail a foiling sailing dinghy with in-line T-foils. Such a boat should not be viewed as requiring basic sailing skills beyond that needed to sail a fast planing dinghy such as a Laser. Sailors of skiffs / asymmetric dinghies or with experience of apparent wind sailing will find the skill set very similar.

The foiling dinghy really is a versatile machine that can span gender as well as a variety of weights, shapes and sizes.

This book will give you an insight into how such boats work and the basic techniques required to sail one confidently and prove that, if you can sail a performance dinghy competently, you can fly!

Learning to foil is a journey that needs to be guided for the beginner. There is a lot involved in learning to foil. The speeds attainable bring with them an obligation to foil responsibly taking into account the safety of yourself and others.

PRE-REQUISITES TO SAIL A FOILING DINGHY

Sailing a foiling dinghy is a continuous learning process that builds on your pre-existing sailing skills: the better you are at sailing a high performance sailing dinghy, the easier it will be to transfer these skills to foiling. The ability to swim used to be essential: foiling can be an immersion sport when you are learning, particularly in Moths but, with the advent of boats such as the F101, this no longer has to be the case!

FITNESS

Most first time Moth sailors will capsize a fair few times on initial sails but again this is not so true on some of the new foilers. Be prepared for a bit of exercise on your first sails as the boat will give every muscle in your body (and your cardiovascular system) a good workout.

Foiling: A cardiovascular workout

BODY ARMOUR

Wear a wetsuit that covers most of your body: this is for protection from bumps and bruises as climbing in and out of the boat will take its toll on the body. Even the best sailors wear a full wetsuit all the time to ensure that they maximise the pleasure and minimise the pain. Good sailing boots that protect the ankle, whilst being flexible and grippy, are ideal; you will also be doing a lot of sail trimming so gloves are a good idea too!

Recommended sailing kit

We also recommend that beginners wear a helmet. When teaching beginners we often use helmets with built-in radio communication in order to give real-time feedback. This accelerates the learning curve for experienced sailors who often have to unlearn many years of different sailing techniques.

However, the helmet should also be considered by the more experienced. Closing speeds of two foiling boats are potentially above 40 mph and, in this context, wearing a helmet seems a sensible precaution when sailing in the company of other foiling boats. Interestingly, the French Sailing Federation has made the wearing of helmets compulsory when racing foiling craft.

Sailing a foiling boat will change your view of sailing forever: you have been warned!

GETTING STARTED

Learning any new skill can be made much easier by using some basic rules that run true for trying most sports. Foiling requires a sound understanding of well-developed sailing skills. If you have not previously mastered sailing a planing dinghy then your learning process is destined to be longer.

I would strongly recommend having lessons in a foiling school of which more and more are starting to spring up as the popularity and awareness of this branch of the sport develops. This has the advantage of learning in someone else's boat (you will find a reluctance of most foiling sailors to lend you their carbon fibre pride and joy). The boat is likely to be set up properly and you will save yourself so much time and potential damage that the cost of the course will be a good investment. Many people have learned the hard way thus far but it does require determination, a good skill set and a substantial financial investment. Learning on a well set up boat, with good tuition in a safe environment prior to buying a foiling dinghy will pay dividends.

Learning at a foiling school is much easier than learning by yourself

Overview: Sailing boats have been foiling since 1939 but the advent of modern materials and sophisticated computer software have allowed significant developments since 2000.

WHERE FOILING STARTED

Hydrofoils are not a recent invention. As long ago as 1861, Thomas Moy conducted model towing tests of hydrofoils in the Surrey canal in England, but his interest was in flying rather than boats and he was only using water as a safer test bed than going up in the sky. In 1897, the Conte de Lambert built a full-scale steam-driven hydrofoil catamaran which reached good speeds on the River Seine. In 1898, Italian engineer Enrico Forlanini started designing hydrofoils and in 1906 he tested an engine-powered hydrofoil on Lake Magiore.

Sailing hydrofoils first appeared in the United States with Robert Gilruth's small foiling catamaran in 1939, and in the 1950s J G Baker built a monohull with large V-foils (2 at the front and 1 at the back). This attracted the attention of the US Navy who funded him to build *Monitor*, a much larger monohull, using two tapered ladder foils and a V-foil at the stern. But the US Navy lost interest and the project stopped.

J G Baker's first foiling boat, built in 1950

J G Baker's second foiling boat, Monitor *in 1955*

Baker was followed by fellow American Don Nigg who developed a series of hydrofoil boats in the 1960s, culminating in *Flying Fish* which was launched in 1968, for which plans were published and several examples built around the world.

Don Nigg's Flying Fish, *launched in 1968*

The mantle for sailing hydrofoil development then transferred to the UK, with James Grogono fitting hydrofoils to his Tornado catamaran *Icarus* which was developed alongside Philip Hansford's *Mayfly*. Both these boats held the World Speed Record for more than 10 years in their respective classes: *Icarus* in 'B' Class and *Mayfly* in 'A' Class.

Also in the 1970s, Frank Raison added V-foils to his wooden scow to create the first foiling Moth which he reported foiled in about 15 knots of wind. However, it didn't like waves and the bow foil was broken in a chop, putting an end to this development.

The materials and manufacturing processes available in the 1970s limited the development of foiling craft both for cost and practical reasons. The foils were difficult and expensive to manufacture and generally heavy, which negated much of the performance gain created by the foils. In fact, for some time, the foiling Tornado, *Icarus*, was beaten at speed trials by a conventional, non-foiling, Tornado catamaran.

However, with the advent of modern materials and appropriate computer software, it became easier to design and build hydrofoils and the development sped up.

James Grogono's foiling Tornado catamaran, Icarus

THE DEVELOPMENT OF THE FOILING MOTH

In 1994, Andy Patterson, of Bloodaxe Boats in the UK, added foils to the International Moth using 3 T-foils in a tripod arrangement – one on each corner of the boat. In 1998 Ian Ward of Australia developed a boat with in-line T-foils with a mechanical sensor controlling the height and this was the first in-line foiling Moth.

Andy Patterson's tripod foiler

Brett Burvill's Trifoiler

The Illet Prowler

In 2000, Brett Burvill reverted to a trifoiler with J-foils mounted from the racks, designed by Mark Pivac. He competed with this in the Moth World Championship in Australia that year and won a race, before it was declared out of class, deemed to be a multihull. Burvill also tried T-foils, but with no auto-control system.

Meanwhile John and Garth Ilett also worked on in-line T-foils, adding a bow-mounted wand to control the ride height in 2002.

They sold their first production boat to Rohan Veal who refined both the boat and the techniques required to sail it, while Ilett tweaked the design.

With a foiling Moth that now 'worked', the Ilett Prowler, and Veal promoting it, the class experienced a renaissance. Having been a somewhat esoteric class, loved by aficionados, but ignored by the majority of sailors, the International Moth suddenly became truly leading edge.

Ilett's company Fasta Craft, could not keep up with demand and soon other manufacturers and designers sought to join in the growth.

Andrew McDougall developed the Bladerider which was manufactured in quantity in China, but lost control of the company and suffered quality problems. He bounced back, working with McConaghy, and created the Mach 2.

Other designers and manufacturers continued to design and build foiling Moths, using all the opportunities for new ideas open to them in a development class.

Bladerider developed by Andrew McDougall

LATEST DINGHY FOILING DEVELOPMENTS

The development of the International Moth into a fully foiling class resulted in an explosion in the popularity of the class to the point where there were more than 200 competitors at the 2017 World Championships in Lake Garda.

It is accepted that, in a development class restricted by fundamental rules, development has necessarily been in a certain direction and where every incremental design improvement comes at a cost. If you take the International Moth rules out of the equation, much more user-friendly and cheaper designs have started to see the light of day.

In terms of cost control we have seen the launch of the Waszp one design by Andrew McDougall. The Waszp still measures as an International Moth but cost has been saved by mass production and the development of extruded foils that can be pushed down like conventional boats and a freestanding rig with innovative boom design.

Clearly, whilst this design has made compromises in terms of making the boats more suitable for mass production and, of course, cost, they are no match on the racetrack for the latest Moth designs such as the Mach 2, Exocet, Rocket and Lennon Thinair designs.

A few designs have more recently developed dinghy foiling away from the confines of the International Moth rules in order to overcome the features of the Moth which make learning more challenging. This has also created foiling opportunities for larger and less agile sailors.

The UFO has been developed in the USA and cost has been aggressively tackled in the design brief whilst also creating a stable platform and, again, an easier launching and landing system. The

In the US, the UFO leads the way in affordable, easy-to-use foiling

The Waszp measures as an International Moth, but is more sturdy and cheaper

UFO uses a 'catamaran' style hull to increase static stability and employs an innovative lightweight rig design.

The F101 has pushed these design concepts even further by using a trimaran concept where the stability of the platform and the length of the hulls have been developed to provide a platform which can handle greater crew weights as well as providing less painful crashes and fewer capsizes. With such a stable platform, and foils that retract, the F101 can also be launched from a trolley without the need to carry the fully rigged boat into full-foil length depth of water before you can enter the boat, as is the case with the International Moth.

As time goes by, other foiling dinghies will no doubt come on the market and it is hard to know which will stand the test of time and which will not.

For example, a Moth-like design, the Onefly from France, is creating some interest. It looks similar to the foiling Moth, but does not measure as a Moth – it is too long for starters. It has a two-part mast, with a mainsail bolt rope, meaning that the sail can be hoisted and dropped easily. Like the Waszp, the mast is unstayed.

The Onefly, bigger than a Moth, but offering one-design racing

The F101, designed to make foiling more accessible

THE POSSIBILITIES

As dinghy foils developed there was an obvious case to adapt existing classes by adding foils. Commercial foils have been made to fit the standard Laser hull and RS Aero. Theoretically, at least, if a foil is pushed through the water at the right angle and enough speed, it can generate enough force to lift most hulls out of the water. Practically, however,

the dinghy needs an appropriate hull and rig if it is to foil in any other direction than pretty much downwind in a full gale. The weight of the hull, the weight and efficiency of the rig and the amount of the all-important righting moment that the original boat has will have a huge effect on a boat's ability to fly. To prove the point, Adam May fitted foils to an Optimist. Clive Everest has also recently attached foils to Cherubs and foils were added to his RS600 design which had a sailing configuration of trapezing on racks whilst foiling: certainly not for the feint-hearted or novice foiler.

RS600 with foils

Foiling Laser with Wildwind

Foiling Cherub at Foiling Week, Lake Garda

Overview: Foils provide lift, like an aeroplane's wing, but need controls to provide lift when required and then to level out the flying height.

THE FOILS

T-FOILS

Hydrofoils for dinghies have really been developed around in-line T-foils. Whilst foiling dinghies have also used other configurations (Cherub, Quant 23, FLO 1), the scope of this book and the techniques we use will focus on the more conventional in-line T-Foils.

The daggerboard and rudder are replaced with 2 vertical foils with horizontal foils on the end

This type of foiling dinghy has two horizontal foiling surfaces, each one of these attached to a vertical foil. One is placed where we would conventionally put the daggerboard and the other on the rudder. The main horizontal foil has an adjustable flap on its trailing edge. The rudder foil has no flap but can generally have its angle of attack changed manually by the sailor on the water via a twist grip in the tiller extension mechanism.

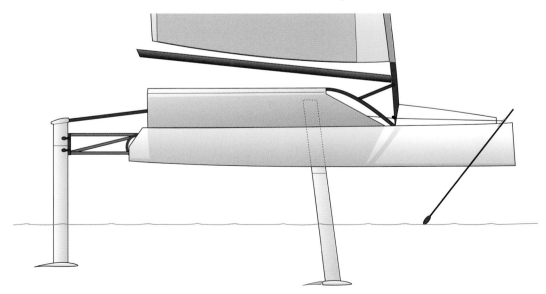

The idea is that the boat lifts up onto these foils (just as an aeroplane takes off using its wings), so the hull is no longer in the water. This reduces the drag and dramatically increases the speed.

The highest speeds can be obtained 'flying' with the hull as high as possible out of the water because this minimises the amount of the foil that is in the water and the drag it causes and can give a much greater righting moment from the sailor's bodyweight. However, as soon as any part of the horizontal foil comes out of the water, the hydrodynamics break down and a wipe-out is likely. So, there is a balance between flying high for speed and flying lower for reliability, stability and safety.

The clever bit is how these foils are controlled to provide lift when required, but to stop providing lift when it would take you too high and possibly out of the water and into a crash.

Hydrofoils do not work well in air: if you fly too high, you will come down with a bump

Front foil coming out of the water means the foiling is over

THE CONTROL SYSTEM

The control wand is typically located at the front of the boat (e.g. International Moth) or attached to the back of the daggerboard (e.g. F101, Laser, Aero). The wand mechanism is a device, which controls the height at which the boat will fly out of the water by adjusting the trailing edge of the main foil (flap), very much like the flaps on an aeroplane wing.

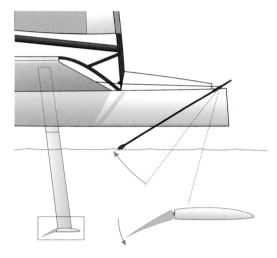

The wand back and the main foil giving full lift

Starting from the bow of the boat this is how it works: When the boat is moving slowly through the water the wand is pushed backwards against the return elastic by water pressure toward the water surface. (On the Moth this elastic is attached to the May stick – a rod that extends beyond the end of the wand to provide enough leverage for the elastic to pull the wand down against the water.) The wand moves a series of push rods that push the flap of the main foil downwards into a position where it will give vertical lift and, if there is enough forward speed, it will generate enough lift to raise the hull out of the water.

As the speed increases and the hull lifts from the water the wand is pulled down to the water surface by the pressure of the elastic. As it 'feels' the distance to the water surface it automatically reduces the angle of the main flap to a neutral position. At this point it stops sending the boat higher and actually levels the boat out at the ride height that the sailor has pre-set before sailing.

If the hull goes further out of the water the wand will be pulled further forwards, pulling the main foil flap past the neutral position into a negative lift situation. This will make the boat return to a flight altitude closer to the water.

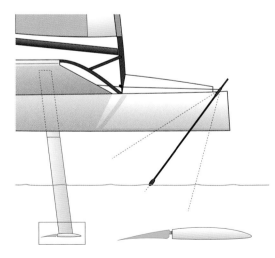

The wand at 45 degrees and the main foil in the neutral position

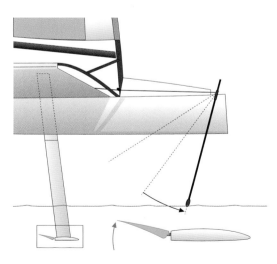

The wand near vertical and the main foil giving negative lift

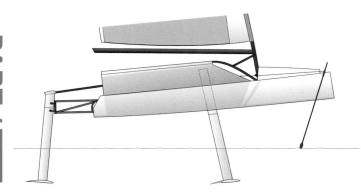

When the rudder is angled backwards, the bow is forced up

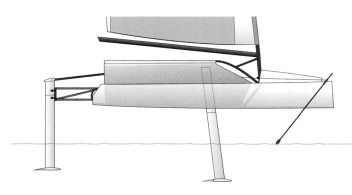

When the rudder is upright, the bow is level

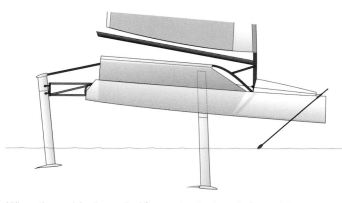

When the rudder is angled forwards, the bow is forced down

RUDDER FOIL ADJUSTMENT

At the rear of the boat the rudder horizontal foil is also creating lift as well as steering the boat like any conventional dinghy. The balance of lift is something the designer will have taken into account when deciding the size and shape of the relative foils and the anticipated crew weight and sailing position so that the boat will lift off and indeed sail at the correct level of pitch in a stable manner. The rudder foil angle can be adjusted whilst sailing by twisting the tiller extension.

Angling the rudder foil forwards underneath the back of the boat increases the angle of attack of the foil and generates more lift. This lifts the back of the boat higher, trims the bow down which decreases the angle of attack of the main foil and reduces its lift. Pushing the rudder foil backwards reduces the lift on the rudder, lifts the bow up and increases the angle of attack of the main foil which gives it more lift.

This adjustment is usually achieved by rotating the tiller extension in a clockwise or anti-clockwise direction. This action drives a worm gearing that lengthens or shortens a rod inside the tiller. This rod moves the rudder stock forwards and backwards as required to control the angle of attack of the rudder foil which controls the amount of lift and thus the fore and aft trim of the boat (also known as pitch).

FOIL SET-UP FOR BEGINNERS

When you first sail a foiling boat it should be set up so that you do not have to worry about the foils: you can just focus on the sailing of the boat. Initially, you would also want to set the height you fly at to a lower level to give a safer, more forgiving ride with a much greater margin for error.

The specific set-up should be covered in your boat manual and is also discussed on p98.

The angle of attack of the main foil is critical. The margin of error is minimal and 0.5 of a degree will have a massive impact on the performance of the foil and how ultimately the boat performs. The angle of attack can be changed in a number of ways:

- *A variety of pin positions can be used in the Moth and Waszp.*
- *An adjustment wheel on the F101 gives infinite possibilities to fine tune.*

In the Moth the position of the pin controls the angle of attack

HEEL OF THE BOAT

There is another fundamental point about the way the foils work that needs to be appreciated by the beginner at this stage. This is the angle of heel of the boat. Most sailing is thought of, explained and taught in 2 dimensions. It is perceived that sailing is mainly focussed on controlling the wind in the sails and the rudder and centreboard just stop the boat slipping sideways through the water and help to steer the boat. To fully grasp foiling you need to think in 3 dimensions as the different forces involved really come into focus when you are controlling foils beneath the water that you cannot even see.

If the boat is heeling to leeward (how many conventional dinghy sailors are comfortable), the angle of the foil in the water, and the forces of leeway upon it, prevents lift being generated and stops the boat from rising up on the foils. However, if the boat is heeled to windward, the angle of the foil in the water, and the forces upon it, creates further lift, and this will help promote foiling at lower speeds.

Sailing upright allows the foils to give lift in the way we have described earlier, but does not give that additional lift which being slightly heeled to windward does. There is also the risk that, if you are sailing upright, a gust will cause you to heel to leeward and therefore stall out the foils. Heeling to windward will also help to increase righting moment. The mind-set is to sail the boat heeled on top of you and bringing it back on top of you immediately it starts to go upright, NOT allowing the boat to heel to leeward and then bring it flat as you might be more used to doing.

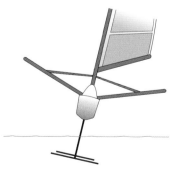

Mast heeled to leeward and foil generating negative lift

Mast upright and foil neutral

Mast heeled to windward and foil generating lift

APPARENT WIND

The speed of boats that you have sailed before will have determined your familiarity with apparent wind. With the increased speeds achieved while foiling, a thorough grasp of the concept of apparent wind is essential.

The word 'apparent' is a good way of describing the direction of the wind indicated by your wind indicator or flag when you are travelling at speed. When a boat is at rest, the direction of the wind indicator is an indication of the true direction of the wind but, as the boat accelerates, its forward movement generates, in effect, a second wind blowing from the front. This second wind and the real wind combine to become the apparent wind.

This can be likened to putting your hand out of a car window when the car is moving: although the true wind may be blowing across the car it will feel as though the wind is blowing from the front because the car is travelling forward through the air.

Once foiling, the apparent wind moves quickly forward

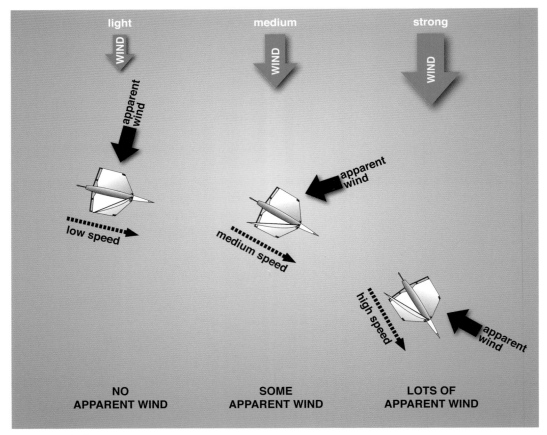

Apparent wind

Spreader / prodder bracket

Forestay

Stay

Mast

Kicking strap

May stick

Hull

Main foil

Wand

Mainsail

Batten

Outhaul

Boom

Mainsheet

Wing

Trampolene

Tiller extension

Tiller

Wing float

Toestrap

Rudder gantry

Rudder & rudder foil

Moth

Mast

Windsurfer boom

Mainsail

Batten

Mainsheet

Outhaul

Wing

Tiller extension

Trampolene

Tiller

Rudder & rudder foil

Wing float

Toestrap

Wand

Main foil

Hull

Rudder gantry

Waszp

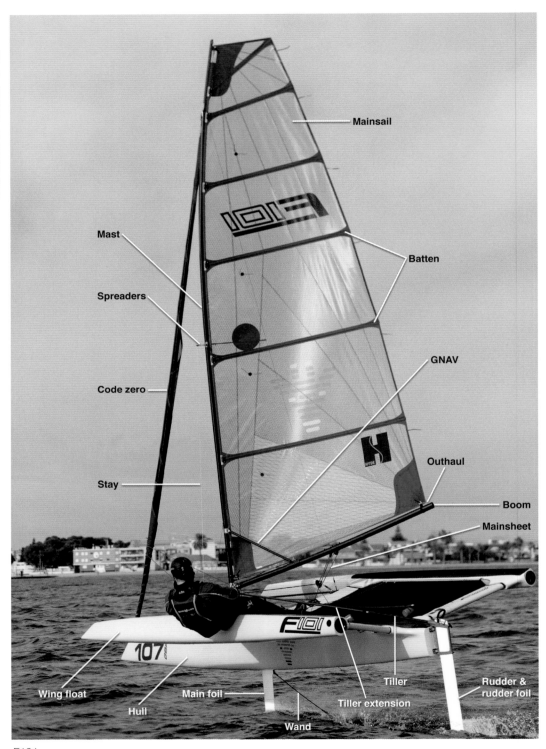

Mainsail

Batten

Mast

Spreaders

GNAV

Code zero

Outhaul

Stay

Boom

Mainsheet

Wing float

Tiller

Rudder & rudder foil

Main foil

Hull

Tiller extension

Wand

F101

Batten

Mast

Mainsail

Jumper-stays

Wish-boom

Jumper-strut

Mainsheet

Wand sprit

Tiller extension

Wand

Main foil
(in front of mast)

Rudder &
rudder foil

Tiller

Hull

Toestrap

UFO

Objective: To set the boat up in preparation for launching.

Overview: Production boats come with a comprehensive rigging guide. Assuming that the boat has all of the standard controls set up according to the rigging guide, we shall cover the basics of getting the boat prepared to go on the water.

RIGGING

Firstly, sleeve the sail on the mast and attach the cams. The sail cams lock in the draft of the sail into the mast and produce a very efficient entry, they can be a bit tricky to attach to the mast. Placing the mast over your knees and pushing down on the cam can often pop it in to place.

The cams lock the sail into the mast

Sleeving the sail on the mast

There are several ways to put your rig on the boat and they will vary depending on whether you have anyone to help, how windy it might be and also your local launching and rigging area. This method assumes you are on your own, although having two people makes the whole operation much simpler.

By placing the boat across the wind (this angle depends on the wind strength and whether you have a helper) you can get the wind to help lift the rig into place: take care here as, if you do not control the rig perfectly, you can damage the hull –

this is a good time to have a friend!

Rig tension and mast rake vary throughout the Moth fleet. With many sailors using canting rigs added to the fully battened camber induced sails which induce mast twist, rig tension should be taken off the forestay. Rake will depend on sailor weight, wind and water conditions but, as a general guide, 4 or 5 on the Loos gauge and enough room so you can get under the boom in a tack is a good place to start. Most modern Moths now use a kinked boom which allows a more comfortable boom height.

1 Attach the downhaul

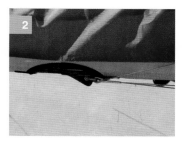

2 Attach the shrouds

3 And the spreader / prodder bracket: I always leave the shrouds attached to the boat

4 Leave sufficient slack on the forestay to allow lifting and seating on the mast step

5 Place the mast in the step and start lifting

6 Pull the mast up wth the forestay

7 Pull the mast upright

8 Tie the forestay to the bow

9 Attach the boom to the sail and mast

WASZP RIGGING

The Waszp sail is sleeved in the same manner as the Moth. The windsurfer boom attachment is unique to the design and there is an extensive manual for the Waszp where you can see exactly how this should be attached. With no rake to adjust on the mast on this boat, the rigging is pretty straightforward if you follow the manual.

The Waszp, because it has no standing rigging, has the advantage over a conventional Moth of being able to allow the mast to rotate all the way to the front of the boat if you release the mainsheet. This is handy for returning to the beach in an onshore wind. It also makes it easier to wheel the boat on the trolley with the sail up

OTHER SET-UP TIPS

When learning, other top tips for setting up your Moth are:

RETURN ELASTIC

The tension on the wand can be adjusted by pulling on the return elastic. How hard this is pulled can have a significant effect on how the foils react to the input of the passing waves. If the return is too tight it can pull the wand down below the water surface at low speeds if the wand end is of insufficient surface area. You can often hear this.

Gravity helps the wand to drop to the water surface once flying but, if the return elastic is too loose, then the wand can skip off the water and this can cause a porpoising effect. So: tight enough to stop the bouncing of the wand, and not so tight that it makes the wand feel every bump in the water. As a rule of thumb you will need more tension in stronger wind conditions, less in the light.

WAND PREVENTER

When you are starting to sail a foiling boat with a bow wand there are times when you often end up, unintentionally, going backwards. This can be stressful on the wand mechanism and can be alleviated by the fitting of a small line to prevent this happening.

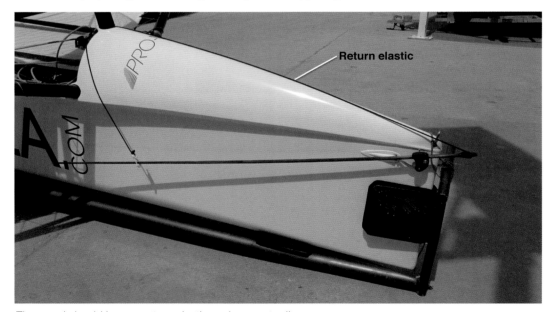

The wand should have a return elastic and preventer line

RIGHTING LINES

Capsizing the Moth when you are learning is an occupational hazard. If you are light, or on the shorter side, then it can be helpful to set up some righting lines on the wing bars. This allows you to lower your centre of gravity when initially righting the boat.

Righting lines in place and about to be used

MAINSHEET

We use a 3:1 ratio mainsheet for the beginner on the Moth. This makes the initial trimming of the mainsheet easier when the loads necessary for sailing upwind are not needed and the sail can be trimmed much more quickly in this configuration. Once you have mastered the art of steering and moving your bodyweight you will need to increase the purchase to enable you to grind on the mainsheet to sail upwind more efficiently.

When learning a 3:1 mainsheet makes trimming easier

SHROUDS

The shrouds can be a place of pain when sailing the Moth as you have a tendency to crash forwards. We would recommend padding out the shrouds and their adjusters.

TILLER ELASTIC

Many in the Moth fleet like a shockcord running across the top of the tiller. This automatically centralises the rudder and, as the rudder sensitivity of foiling boats is so critical, it is certainly worth considering.

Padded shroud

Pad out and tape up the shrouds

Elasticating the tiller helps to keep it centralised

RIG SET-UP

Assuming that you have rigged the boat with a suitable mast rake and rig tension for the conditions (this can normally be obtained from the manufacturer's guide), the boat should be ready to launch. However, if you are sailing a boat that you need to carry into the water (i.e. a Moth), it is important that, as soon as you get in the boat after launching and righting, the sail is set up so that you can sail off immediately.

For your first time in the boat the kicking strap (vang), downhaul and outhaul must be set BEFORE you right the boat ready for sailing. If you have to start worrying about sail setting this will certainly distract you from the more important job in hand of balancing and sailing the boat.

For your first sail you should be looking to be sailing in perfect foiling conditions for beginners: between 8-12 knots; any less it is difficult for the beginner to develop initial stability and any more, well, even the really talented will have a bit on!

Anyone who has used a modern windsurfing or cat rig will know what you are looking to achieve with the set-up as the rig depends a lot on the downhaul tension. If you are a conventional dinghy or keelboat sailor, as a basic guide, you would look to set the downhaul much harder than you would on a normal boat and, likewise, the kicker (vang),

If you have the rig set up like this you will be in the right ball park

with the outhaul adjusted to follow the curve of the bottom batten and not so tight that lines appear between the clew and the tack.

Downhaul really tight

Kicking strap really tight

Outhaul not so tight

Rig settings

GETTING TO THE LAUNCH AREA

Now that the boat itself is rigged it is nearly time to get the foils in. The launching trolley is an integral part of the modern Moth and it has been designed to attach to the boat as you roll the hull and rig over onto its side.

To prepare for this, wheel the boat to a good launching area as close to the water as you can. Moving the boat on the trolley must be done at close angles to the wind or it will simply blow over. You often end up 'tacking' the boat to get to your destination and again, if you have a wing man with their hand on the windward wing, then this makes it all the easier.

Before rolling the boat over on its trolley it is really important to think about your launch and sailing exit from the beach. Launching and landing are the most stressful parts for the first few times out, so give yourself the best chance of success and the least stress possible. A little bit of pre-planning here will save you problems later.

Give yourself plenty of room to leeward of an obstruction

Give yourself plenty of room to leeward of any obstruction. This is because the Moth is likely to luff up as soon as we pull it up from the capsized position and thus take away our opportunity to keep clear of upwind obsructions.

Having selected our area, we put the boat head to wind and lock off the mainsheet using a slip knot as shown.

Now, ensure the battens are rotated and, by gently bearing the bow away from the wind, we roll the boat over onto the leeward wing. We always pad out the wing to prevent damage to the carbon as the boat will spend quite a lot of time on its side. Once the boat is over, rotate the rig and hull until the wind is pushing on the wings at right angles as you do not want the wind lifting the boat upright once the foils are on! You will also find that, if the battens are inverted, the rig will have a tendency to lift the hull. Make sure that the battens are as in the photo here.

Lock off the mainsheet using a slip knot

On its side with the wind at right angles to the wings

FITTING THE FOILS

With the Mach 2 Moth you should always put the rudder on first: the weight of the rudder pulls the balance point of the boat further backward so the boat will sit better once you have removed the trolley. Put the rudder foil in the rudder stock and secure it with the pin.

The key point at this stage is to take the trolley off! The trolley does not come off so easily (though not impossible) once the main foil is in: you just look a bit of a numpty and you will be unable to convince anyone that you meant to do it! Also remember to take off your foil covers: you would not be the first to launch with them on!

Fitting the rudder foil to the Mach 2

Take the trolley off before fitting the main foil

To insert the main foil:

1 Position the main foil

2 Slide in the main foil

3 Release wand so that it drops down

4 Push the foil pin into place

5 Attach the push rod wand linkage

6 Put the wand return elastic on (I run mine around the king post)

FOIL SET-UP

A Mach 2, or other production Moth, should arrive with the foil set up in the right ball park. To set up the angle of attack on the main foil there are 3 holes on the hull side of the main foil pin. The middle one is a good place to start but, if you think you want more lift, use the back hole and, if you want less, then use the front one.

To roughly check the ride height that you have selected, or the set-up on your boat, place the main foil flap in neutral. With the foil flap in neutral, the wand should be at approximately the angle in the middle photograph. You can see that the boat should fly with the foil at that distance under the water. When you are learning there are no extra points for flying too high and a conservative height should be set with a greater margin for error. As you improve you will be more confident and can wind the ride height up.

The flap giving maximum lift (wand back)

The rudder foil should be set with the vertical rudder pin set towards the front of the slot – i.e. with the foil angled forwards underneath the hull (every boat is different, but this is a good starting point to prevent the boat lifting into orbit). This is done by twisting the tiller extension. Initially it is easy to forget which way to wind the tiller so either draw on the side of the boat (it is different on each tack so you will need a picture on both sides) or mark your rudder stock with arrows by the rudder pin as a reference.

The flap in neutral, for maximum speed (wand in neutral position)

Set the rudder foil so the pin is all the way forwards

The flap giving negative lift (and the wand forward)

PRE-FLIGHT CHECKS

Get into the habit of systematically checking your boat before launching. A good method is to start at the bottom and work up!

1. Check that the wand is operating the main flap without friction and that, when the main flap is in neutral, the wand is indicating a ride height as seen in the middle photo on the previous page. Also make sure that you have removed your foil covers!

2. Check all foil attachments are securely fitted and unlikely to break. Ensure all push rods are secure.

3. Make sure that the bungs are in. In the Mach 2 these are small holes drilled in the hull on the starboard stern and king post bulkheads. Simply tape over the top of the holes.

4. Ensure that the rig is suitable for the conditions BEFORE launching. Check rake and that you have enough kicker, downhaul and outhaul to sail off immediately you right the boat.

5. It is essential that you are wearing appropriate protective clothing and a suitable buoyancy aid. Foiling is an immersion sport when you are learning.

6. Always carry a safety knife. I keep mine in my buoyancy aid pocket rather than taped to the tiller (or similar). I can always reach it there should I twist my foot in the bridle or hiking strap, and no-one can nick it!

7. Do not sail alone, tell someone where you are going, when you will be back and what to do if you are late.

Make sure you are familiar with the ABC of foiling safety (see p101).

At Pro-Vela we always use a RIB when teaching beginners for safety, coaching, resting and easy take-offs!

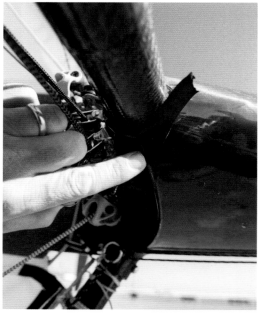

Tape the holes up on the stern and king post bulkheads

LAUNCHING

With all of the pre-flight and safety checks taken care of it is time to launch. Choose your spot carefully as a bit of preparation and thinking will save potential stress later as we detailed earlier. Make sure that you have clear in your mind the direction you want to walk with the boat, its final, planned destination and the relation to the wind. Ideally you should walk with the rig downwind of the hull to ensure the sail is not lifted, the hull righted and the expensive foils damaged.

Approach the boat from the stern, duck under the mainsheet and, with your hands placed as in the photo, you should keep your back straight and your knees bent as you find the perfect balance point before lifting the Moth into the air and walking carefully forwards into the water. If you do have help here it is best deployed at the mast head to

prevent wearing the sail by scraping it along the ground. However, be careful to keep the mast tip as low to the ground as possible as this will help maintain the balance of the boat and stop the lower wing hitting the feet of the sailor.

Once you are in the water up to your hips you can lower the boat onto its wing float.

Your final bit of preparation is to get the mainsheet and tiller ready for when you enter the boat.

At this stage, you may also need to equalise the pressure between the air inside the hull and outside (venting). In some Moths, particularly black ones like the Mach 2, the temperatures can allow a pressure or vacuum to build up in the hull which, respectively, might cause the boat to expand and damage it, or the water to be sucked into the hull. You may also choose to do this after you have been

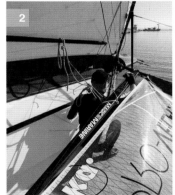

Picking up & carrying the boat into the water

Take the knot out of the mainsheet and place it over the hiking strap

Place the tiller extension on top of the boom

sailing for a bit (particularly in a hot climate). Simply uncover the air hole by removing the tape, release or let in the air, and then put the tape back to re-seal the hole. Some boats now have venting valves fitted.

You can now walk round so that you are in front of the main foil and carry the boat out further into the water so that is deep enough to cover the main foil. Unless you are particularly small, a water depth of shoulder height is a good general guide.

Walk the boat out to a shoulder-height depth

ENTERING THE BOAT (LEG-OVER METHOD)

Firstly, you need to get up onto the main foil. Whilst you do need to take care of the foils, they are built of carbon and so are pretty tough, but you should respect the sharp edges and joints. The main hull, however, can easily be dented so a health warning here: knees and elbows will dent the hull so keep any pressure on the foils and hard chines / edges of the boat.

The hull may initially be floating on the leeward wing float: pull the boat down into the water by the main foil vertical and it should lie just along the top of the water. Keep close to the hull so that you do not bring the boat upright prematurely. You may use your foot against the horizontal foil to help keep your bodyweight close to the hull and push up so

that you can stand up with both feet on the vertical foil. Place the front foot on the hull chine being careful not to stand on the hull.

Drop your bottom whilst holding the wing with both hands. The timing on this next bit, as in righting any capsized boat, is the key: swing the rear leg too late and you end up in the water holding the wing; swing the leg too early and the boat gently returns the rig to the water. Timing it perfectly relies on the fact that you need to watch the leeward wing starting to rid itself of water. This is a bit like carrying a tea tray full of water: once it gets moving it accelerates quickly so you need to carefully manage the rate at which you right the boat and time your leg lift accordingly.

Entering the boat using the leg-over method

As the boat comes upright, swing the rear leg over the wing bar keeping your body close to the wing and your head facing forwards, roll horizontally into the boat and slide your rear foot into the centre of the hull, and your front leg with knee bent to just above the hiking strap.

Ensure that the leeward wing is pushed on to the wing float, but not under the water, so the boat is heeled to leeward. If you followed your pre-flight preparation you should find the mainsheet and tiller extension right where you want them. Take hold of the tiller and mainsheet.

Leg-over in a two-man boat

It should be noted that, if it becomes windier, it is more difficult to reach in for the mainsheet and tiller extension without capsizing. If this happens, it is possible to rest the windward wing in the water. The windage on the rig is able to be balanced by your weight and the windward heel.

ALWAYS go for the tiller extension first. If you can steer the boat to a beam reach position you will have a greater success rate when looking to pick up the mainsheet from the hiking strap.

LAUNCHING TROUBLESHOOTING

Problem	Cause	Solution
The boat won't come up	Lack of righting force	Use righting lines, step back on the vertical foil.
Boat bears away and then capsizes	The windward wing is in the water and the rig forces will turn the boat off the wind	Pull the boat up slowly: make sure the leeward wing stays in / on the water. Get your leg over / in the boat earlier. Get the tiller under control and push it away firmly as you get in the boat.
Boat capsizes again	Not enough force being applied for long enough	You are getting in the boat too early. Timing is everything. Make sure the water tension is broken on the leeward trampoline.
Boat flops on the windward wing	Too much weight to windward	Make sure the back foot gets down to the centreline. The chances are that you entered the boat too late. Timing is everything.

Objective: To set the boat up in preparation for launching.

Overview: The F101 has a more conventional rig set up with a stayed mast, which remains upright when not in use, and the mainsail is pulled up the mast by a halyard. This has the advantage that, if you wish to launch or land with an onshore or offshore breeze, you have the ability to drop your mainsail. It is also much easier to place the boat where you want prior to going sailing or between flights.

The F101 is also the only foiling boat currently that has a code zero. This is also hoisted by halyard and then furled onto a continuous furling drum.

The boat comes with a comprehensive rigging guide which will tell you how to step the mast and give you the correct basic rig set up in terms of rake and rig tensions.

The foils are also permanently positioned in the boat, so this just needs to be done at the start of the season or after trailing. They are designed to remain fully up ashore and then lowered when in the water for sailing. Again, the rigging guide will tell you all you need to know about getting them in place.

For this book we have assumed that you have followed these instructions and the mast is up, the code zero hoisted and the foils in.

Ashore, the F101 is stored with its mast up and foils in

MAIN FOIL SET-UP

The F101 has a wheel system to control ride height and a further wheel that can adjust the angle of attack on the main foil. Accurate basic settings can be found from the manufacturer's guide but, in basic terms, the foil can be set up in much the same way as the Moth foil prior to putting it into the boat. Check the wand position is at the height you would like to fly at and then check the main flap is in a neutral position at this point. If it is not, adjust the top wheel until you reach the desired position. Once the foil is set up as desired you can insert it into its foil box.

On your first set up we would find a nice soft, flat area and with plenty of padding and a helper, capsize the boat on its trolley, remove the trolley and insert the foil and check it is working as you want it. This will also help you get a good understanding of how the systems function.

A wheel behind the daggerboard, adjusted by the red rope, controls the angle of attack of the foil

A box on top of the daggerboard, adjusted by the red rope, controls the ride height

If the rope is pulled, the ride height is changed

RUDDER FOIL SET-UP

As with the Moth we would recommend that you start your rudder with the pin towards the front of its box. This will make sure the bow is down initially when you go out for your first flight. You can then add lift to the front foil as you become more confident.

The boat manual should also give you a good starting point for this setting.

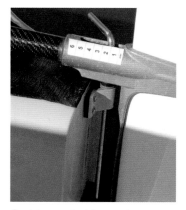

Rudder angled forwards

Rudder angled back

Rudder foil locking nut

PART 2

47

GETTING TO LAUNCH AREA

The F101 can easily be moved to the launch area as the mainsail is not raised at this point, so there is not the need to keep the bow pointing towards the wind all the time.

RIGGING

Once the F101 has been wheeled to the launching area it should be placed head to wind to hoist the mainsail.

The furling code zero would already be set up but it is only really necessary in the lower wind ranges.

Care should be taken to set the boom on the appropriate side of the pre-inserted main foil. This can be ascertained by working out which way you want to sail away from the beach according to the prevailing wind conditions.

PRE-FLIGHT CHECKS

The F101 is simpler than the Moth in terms of pre-flight checks as the launching should be a lot less fraught as it is much more user-friendly in a low-riding mode. Having previously checked the foils are working and positioned correctly you need to ensure that they are locked in the up position with the elastic on the main foil and the rudder stock wing nuts on the rudder. The mainsail should be hoisted with careful attention being payed to which side of the main foil that you will set the boom on.

F101s ready to launch

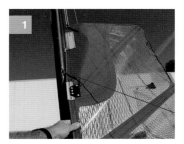

1 Attach the main halyard and feed the mainsail into the track

2 Feed the sail into the track

3 Pull the sail up with the main halyard

4 When fully up, put the halyard in the cleat

5 Tidy away the halyard in the bag

6 ...so the ropes are neat and tidy

LAUNCHING

The F101 is a light-weight fully carbon boat that has been optimised for foiling in lighter wind ranges. Finding a suitable launching / landing area is absolutely key to enjoy your foiling boat to the maximum with the minimum amount of stress. A gently shelving slipway would be the perfect launching site and launching and landing with the help of a friend or crewmate would be recommended.

Launching a foiling boat in waves should be avoided. Most incidents that could damage your boat will happen within 50 metres of the beach during the launch and landing process so taking time to plan these aspects of your sailing session is essential.

With the foils in their 'ashore' position, protruding slightly from the bottom of the boat, the F101 should be pushed gently backwards into sufficient water to float the boat comfortably off the trolley so that the main foil does not catch on the rear support of the trolley. To do this we would put one person on the windward float whilst the other person releases the trolley tie downs. The boat should then float off backwards into deep enough water so that, when the boat drops onto one of the floats: no damage to the foils will be possible.

Ideally the windward float will now be in the water enabling the crew to lower the foils into a position which gives enough steering and lateral resistance to sail the boat into a location where the foils can be fixed fully down into position in preparation for foiling.

If you are going to need to tack to get there, then you will also need to ensure the foils are far enough down to ensure the boom can pass over the top of the main foil.

1 Wheel the boat into the water

2 To a depth where you can float the boat off the trolley

3 Float the boat off the trolley

4 Return the trolley to the shore

5 Lower the rudder to a suitable depth

6 And similarly for the main foil

THE SECURE POSITION

Objective: To attain a stable platform from which you can make the transition into the sailing position.

Overview: This position is the basis of any further progress. The basic techniques of this hold true for both the Moth and Waszp but there are small differences for the F101. The key points are:
- Leeward wing float pressed against the water (as described when entering the Moth – see p44).
- Your bodyweight should be over the main hull with the body in a dynamic position.

This body position is also known as the 'Meerkat' and will be used extensively as you progress to transitions on the foils so learn it well, it is one of the keystones of foiling and you will use it frequently all through your foiling life:
- Back foot over centreline
- Front knee bent
- Front shoulder level with mainsheet
- Tiller held across in front of your body
- Mainsheet in your tiller hand fingers (your front hand should be free to act as a support, a push-off point and mainsheet trim as required).

The Meerkat position – a keystone of foiling

So, with the body in the Meerkat and the boat balanced against the leeward wing float you have achieved the 'secure position'. The Moth has a VERY narrow hull and balancing it will appear at first to be like walking on a tight rope or riding a bike. The key concept to grasp is that, just like tightrope walkers or kids on bikes, you need to balance the forces. With wing floats you have been given some stabilisers and it is by balancing against these that the beginner will have the confidence to move quickly into flight mode.

Stable in the secure position and the leeward wing float in the water

KEY POINTS

1 The boat should be laying in a beam reach position.

2 Make sure the tiller is in front of you, across your lap and over the mainsheet.

3 The mainsheet should be held by the little finger in the back 'tiller' hand closest to the mainsheet block.

SECURE POSITION TROUBLESHOOTING

Problem	Cause	Solution
Boat flops to windward	Too much weight to windward	Make sure the back leg is over the centreline, weight pushing down and to leeward.
Boat capsizes to leeward	Too much weight to leeward	Makes sure the leeward wing is not under the water. If it is only the float that is on the water you will find the surface tension will stabilise the boat. Once the trampoline is covered by water it is easy for the boat to capsize again.

DIFFERENCES FOR THE F101

The F101 has been designed to work in a different way from the Moth in that, to start foiling, you need to have the boat leaning on the windward float and main hull with the leeward float in the air. This design feature is to counteract the sailor's natural tendency to sail the boat heeled to leeward which stalls the foils and prevents them from lifting the boat. Whilst this will feel a bit odd to begin with there is sufficient volume in the boat to support the sailor's weight in this position. The Meerkat position is still key, and the boat set up with the windward hull in the water will actually see the boat sitting comfortably in a resting position, from here it is a simple transition to the sailing position.

The secure position in the F101

Objective: Move from the secure position to the sailing position to achieve confident low riding.

Overview: From the secure position you need to transfer your weight out into a sitting position on the wing bar. This must be done in co-ordination with balancing the power in the rig by pulling in the mainsheet. (Note: The sheet and tiller should be held in the rear hand as you may, at times, want to use your front hand to balance.)

This position is common for all the foiling boats with no major differences for the Moth, Waszp or F101. The F101 has a much more stable platform and can rest on either the leeward or windward floats and any errors will not result in a capsize so skills can be learned much quicker.

With the boat sitting on a course somewhere between close-hauled and a beam reach, in one movement you can sheet in, sit out on to the wing bar and then balance the boat solely by trimming the power in the mainsheet. (It is vital at this point to choose a goal point to steer towards and help maintain your focus. Once the boat has accelerated and you are sailing on apparent wind it is very easy to become 'wind blind'.)

Your body should be positioned just behind the mainsheet. (Avoid the armchair position, with both legs bent at the knees and perpendicular to the centreline. This is such a difficult posture to move from if the boat heels on top of you: your ankles become higher than your knees, your knees higher than your hips and gravity will ensure that the boat will eventually capsize to windward. A dynamic position is essential.)

Use the front foot to push down on the hiking strap (this is a most useful part of the boat as it can be used to push off, pull on and generally stop you sliding all over what is a usually slippery trampoline). The back foot can then move up and out and slip underneath the hiking strap with the body weight out on the wing bar. The shoulders should be facing in the direction of travel and the front foot on top of the hiking strap. Using a 3-point contact of both feet and one hand will give the most stable position.

The sailing position

The tiller will keep the rear hand busy so holding the mainsheet and balancing will employ the front hand.

At this stage it is very easy to 'put your head into the boat': looking at your feet, the mainsheet, tiller etc., etc. rather than looking at where you are going. The latter is fundamental to success so, again, remember to choose a goal point to sail at and stick to it. Small variations in the steering have a huge impact on the power control in the rig. It is very easy to become disoriented so keeping on course is vital to avoid getting yourself in a position where you are likely to capsize and an energy-sapping recovery becomes inevitable.

Many sailors, who are new to trying an unstable boat, seem to have a natural reaction to 'pull on everything' as soon as the boat heels to leeward. But moving your body weight out as soon as the boat heels to leeward results in sheeting in and bearing away, thus increasing the chances of a capsize. The more this happens, the greater the temptation to hike and the worse things become. Simply ease the mainsheet OR steer slowly towards the wind to de-power. Keep your head out of the boat and just sail it like a normal small sailing dinghy.

If you begin to heel to leeward, ease the mainsheet or steer slowly towards the wind to de-power

If you begin to heel to windward, pull the tiller towards you and sheet in

Likewise, when the boat heels to windward the natural temptation is to move the bodyweight into the boat: doing this eases the mainsheet and pushes the tiller away as you move in and this turns the boat into the wind, completely de-powering the rig and results in a windward capsize.

To ensure that you can control the steering and sheeting it is essential that the mainsheet is UNDERNEATH the tiller extension. This will enable you to escape the windward capsize as you can lift the arms up which can pull the tiller towards you, bearing the boat away from the wind and powering up, at the same time as pulling the sheet in harder. If the wing does not lift at this stage then move the tiller around the back of the boom, onto the leeward wing and bring the body weight into the centre of the boat to a secure (Meerkat) position with the leeward wing pushed down against the water.

BODY MANAGEMENT

Maintaining a dynamic body position is key to success at this stage. Sit central in the boat to maintain the fore and aft trim. Moving the body weight fore and aft will change the angle of attack of the main foil and have a major influence on the performance of the foils. To keep the variables to a minimum, keep the boat flat fore and aft.

TILLER MANAGEMENT

Place the tiller over your lap in front of you, holding it in your thumb and forefinger with fingers ready to aid sheeting.

MAINSHEET MANAGEMENT

The sheet MUST be held underneath the tiller.

The tiller should be in front on you, held between the thumb and forefinger with the other fingers holding the mainsheet

Sailing with the leeward wing just out of the water will at this stage build confidence, as the confidence grows you can sail the boat more upright, always maintaining a still body, steering a straight course towards your goal point and adjusting the balance of the boat ONLY by trimming in and out on the mainsheet. TRIM TO BALANCE THE BOAT.

You will quickly build confidence in increasing and decreasing power by sail trimming and SMALL tiller movements and SMALL body movements. With so many variables to control the balance of the boat we should focus initially on trimming, trimming and more trimming. As a coach the two most commonly used words for beginners are 'ease' and 'trim' and

the ability to do these quickly and smoothly will be the key to having a steep learning curve.

As you get better and more confident you will build small adjustments into the steering, and bodyweight changes which will minimise the gross movements of trimming you will do initially.

One of the BIG issues with learning on the Moth and Waszp is that the telltales stick to sail when wet (and, when you are learning, they are ALWAYS wet). Telltales on the shrouds often stick to the shrouds and wind indicators normally get trashed within 5 minutes of putting them on, so it is acknowledged that sail trimming is REALLY hard when learning and it is a skill that you need to learn as it is all about 'feel'. Wind blindness is real and steering to a goal point will help massively in the learning stages.

KEY POINTS

1 No hiking, do not use bodyweight.
2 Steer straight, choose goal point.
3 Trim and ease, trim and ease, trim and ease to keep the boat flat.
4 Practise sailing position to secure position transitions.
5 Practise recovery from windward wing dip.
6 Watch for the water on the tea tray / wing. (This is where the trampoline is underwater and will weigh the boat down. As soon as the boat heels more to windward the water will rapidly disperse with a quick release and the sailor's bodyweight will generate a fast roll onto the windward side. Release the water slowly so you are not caught out.)

USEFUL DRILLS

Even if there is not enough wind to foil, time spent in the boat is essential in order to practise the balancing skills required to sail a Moth. The skill set required in terms of tiller and mainsheet management are very similar to a standard Laser as the steering and sail sheeting layout is essentially the same. Sailing in tight circles (in both directions) will enable you to practice the key skills of rapid sheeting and easing whilst steering with the dagger grip at the same time.

SAILING POSITION TROUBLESHOOTING

Problem	Cause	Solution
Boat capsizes to windward	Not enough power, too much weight to windward	Trim the sail correctly, focus on steering towards your goal point.
Boat capsizes to leeward	Too much power, not enough weight to windward	Trim the sail correctly, focus on steering towards your goal point.

DIFFERENCES FOR THE F101

The sailing position is more comfortable in the F101 because, with either wing in the water, the boat is quite stable and so it is less of the balancing act required in the Moth.

The sailing position in the F101

Objective: To sail the boat away from the shore.

Overview: As with any boat, sailing away from a shore with a cross-wind is relatively easy, although the foils do add an extra complication. Sailing away with offshore or onshore winds is more difficult and needs to be thought through beforehand. The Moth requires a 'wet' launch, the F101 must be trolley launched and the Waszp can do both methods to some extent.

SAILING OFF IN A MOTH / WASZP (WET LAUNCH, NO TROLLEY, FOILS DOWN)

CROSS-SHORE WIND

This is without doubt the most favoured wind direction for sailing off or back to shore in any boat and the Moth is certainly no different. As long as there is enough depth of water this is as stress-free a launch as the Moth will ever provide. Right the boat remembering it will have a tendency to shoot forwards as it comes up. Using the 'leg-over' (see p43) or 'waterstart' (see p75) method, enter the boat and achieve the secure position. Slowly sheet in and low ride to your preferred location for foiling. If only we all sailed from gentle shelving beaches with perfect cross-shore winds every time we wanted to sail!

OFFSHORE WIND

The offshore wind is probably the next best possibility after the cross-shore departure. This can be complicated by a narrow channel to exit from but, in general, the complications will only arise from it being more challenging to balance the power in the rig to maintain a stable run out to the foiling area. Remember again that the boat will turn up wind as you get in, so make sure you have given

yourself enough room to right the boat, get yourself organised, balanced and rounded up before you have grounded your foils.

If you choose the leg-over method then the boat will be more difficult to bear away with the leeward wing in the water (and the rig wanting to turn you up into the wind). You may need to confidently bring the windward wing down to the water to initiate the bear away but this is a skill that is best avoided on your first trip out ... it will be straightforward enough as soon as you have spent some hours in the boat.

The waterstart method has the advantage of having the windward wing in the water so the boat will have a tendency to bear away. It will not give you much time, however, so you do need to be in control of the tiller as you enter the boat.

ONSHORE WIND

This launching option is, without doubt, to be avoided when in the initial stages of learning. It is generally accompanied by the bumpiest water conditions and, if at all constrained by shallows or a channel requiring lots of short tacking, can be a scenario that will provide a lot of challenges.

Swimming the Moth into sufficient water is the first challenge as the wind and any wave activity will be pushing you back onto the beach. IT IS A COMMON MISTAKE TO GET INTO THE BOAT TOO EARLY / TOO SHALLOW. It takes a long time or a lot of money to get your foils back in good condition.

The leg-over entry method will give you a little boost closer to the wind as you bring it up and, if you get in with the boat heeled onto the leeward hull, it will give you the best chance of keeping the boat as close-hauled as you can manage. Get the tiller and mainsheet under control as quickly as possible because, if you are constrained by a channel, you will need to tack under as little stress as possible. A failed or poor tack will see you back on the beach, from where you started, with further potential for foil damage in shallow water. This is why, when teaching new foilers, we always introduce tacking BEFORE foiling: it is a key core skill.

Sailing off in a Waszp

SAILING OFF IN AN F101 / WASZP (TROLLEY LAUNCH AND FOILS UP)

The F101's retractable foils, furling headsail and main halyard make it easier to sail off than a Moth in certain scenarios as you can enter the boat in shallower water and you have a variety of sail options, but it is still a challenging manoeuvre which requires thinking about. The Waszp can also be launched using this method.

CROSS-SHORE WIND
Again, this is the preferred wind direction. As long as the mainsail has been set up on the correct side of the main foil during launching, then it is quite straightforward. The boat is best entered from the windward side. If you are sailing single-handed then you can slide head first into the boat, and then move to the back of the boat and begin pushing the rudder foil down and locking it in position with the butterfly nut. (As soon as the boat moves forwards the lift generated

Sailing off in an F101

by the rudder foil is enough to push it back up out of the water and tricky to steer if you do not secure it initially with the butterfly nut and then with the pin when fully down.) If there is a long shallow area then the foil can only be maintained in this half down position if you go very slowly. The Waszp has a line and cleat system on the rudder so you can also lock it off at a variety of depths.

OFFSHORE WIND
This wind direction is actually more straightforward in terms of managing the launching trolley. The boat will slide easily off the rear of the trolley and the water state should be fairly flat which all aids an easy launch. Just make sure that you have remembered to rig the mainsail on the correct side of the foil so that the boom falls away to the leeward side as you bear away and sail off from the shore.

Make sure you have enough depth of water to deploy the foils sufficiently so that you can steer the boat and the boom will pass over the top of the

main foil. As in the cross-shore launch, turn the bow of the boat away from the wind and steer onto a run. Depending on the wind strength you can deploy the zero which will help turn the bow downwind.

ONSHORE WIND
As with the Moth, this launching option is best avoided when in the initial stages of learning. As said previously, it is generally accompanied by the bumpiest water conditions and, if you are at all constrained by shallows or a channel requiring lots of short tacking, can be a scenario that will provide a lot of challenges.

Sailing with a limited depth of foils in the water adds to the difficulty to making ground upwind as well as tacking. Making sure your rig is set up correctly will help here, having enough kicking strap (vang) on will help but make sure you can drive the boat up to speed to make the foils work or you will just end up going sideways. Sitting well forward in the boat will also stop it slipping sideways.

Objective: To turn the boat around passing through the wind.

Overview: At this stage we are ready to go sailing but, before we fly off to the horizon, we first need to discuss how we are going to slow the boat down, turn the boat around and sail back. We always teach this on land first as the mainsheet, tiller and body management may be somewhat different depending on what boats you have previously sailed.

There are actually very few differences in the tacking and gybing techniques between foiling and conventional boats. The basic skills that are required are the same, they just need to be executed with the tiller and mainsheet configuration that we use in the Moth: a centre mainsheet, coupled with a single long tiller extension that will not go through the middle of the boat past the mainsheet (though many will try) so must, by necessity, pass around the back of the boat.

The Waszp has a transom mainsheet bridle and a forward-mounted mainsheet take off that sets up its own challenges but does allow the tiller extension to pass through the centre of the boat as it is impossible for it to go around the stern. The F101 actually allows both methods.

THE LOW-RIDING TACK: MOTH

PRE REQUISITE POSITIONS, TRANSITIONS AND PROCESS
Positions

The dagger grip on the tiller *The pan handle grip on the tiller* *Steering behind your back*

Transitions

1. Pan handle to dagger grip transition (the finger walk)

The finger walk from pan handle grip to dagger grip

2. The hand switch (tiller and sheet swap)

The hand switch

Process

The following pages show the tacking process on land and water in photographs, but the basic technique is:

- Move the rear foot out from under the hiking strap onto the other side of the boat. (Pay attention to move the foot forwards! As you will need to pivot around this foot, if you move it straight across the boat you will end up with your body at the back of the boat on the new tack.)
- Push the tiller hard over very positively.
- Take the tiller extension around the back of the boat. (Note the Waszp tiller extension will pass through the middle.)
- Tap the tiller extension on the gunwale and hold it there with an open palm.
- Move across the boat and as you do, grab the falls of the mainsheet and tug them (this helps to tack the battens and pull the bow through the wind onto the new tack).
- Adopt the secure (Meerkat) position on the new windward side, steering behind your back (with the pan handle grip) and with the mainsheet in your aft hand.
- ONLY move to the sailing position when you are comfortably established on the other tack...

These are skills that should be intuitive for the foiling sailor, but if they are not executed with confidence the transitions will result in a high percentage of capsizes which result in slow progress as you advance on to foiling transitions. We always go through these on land on a simulator (any dinghy) before going out.

TOP TIP

The Moth will ONLY tack through 90 degrees when you are low riding. If you are not sailing close-hauled with speed BEFORE you tack, the boat will get stuck head to wind (in irons) and you will generally end up wet. If you dip the original leeward wing in the water before you go head to wind then the tack will most likely fail. Far better to roll the boat on top of you (like a roll tack) to dip the old original windward wing in the water which will help with the rotation through the tack. The other plus is that, when you pass through the wind and move your body weight to the new side, rolling the boat to windward will help push the boat more quickly on to the new tack.

TACKING SEQUENCE ON LAND

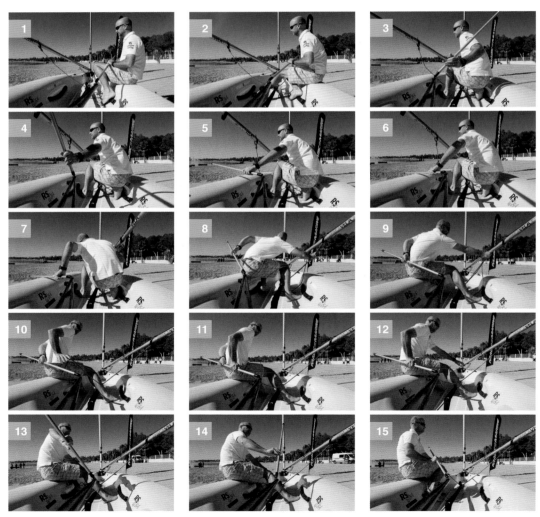

Practising the tacking process on land

TACKING SEQUENCE ON THE WATER

The process is the same as practised on land, with the additional complication of being on an unstable boat! So, in more detail:

- Preparation: If the boat is in a foiling mode, the boat should be slowed and sailed in a low riding mode. (This is achieved by slowly luffing the boat and gently heeling the boat to leeward to stall the foils and bring the hull back down to the water. This will allow the apparent wind to go back towards true wind and thus help to narrow the tacking angle. As mentioned previously, many initial tacks fail as the boat is low riding and NOT sailing close-hauled, thus leaving too great an arc for the boat to travel through and resulting in being stuck in irons.)
- Once the boat is stable the manoeuvre is initiated by body weight and the boat is steered to compensate and maintain stability.
- Move the back foot into the middle of the boat (Meerkat – making sure that the foot moves forwards: it is going to become the front foot) in the secure position and de-power by luffing gently into the wind to maintain a stable platform (the steering / weight relationship is key).
- Push the tiller firmly away and move body weight to maintain the boat in a horizontal plane (more often than not you will dip a wing but try to avoid this as it will kill the boat speed and the chances of a successful turn). If you are going to dip a wing it is much better to be moving uphill through the boat so make sure the old windward wing is more likely to hit the water first.
- Swing the tiller extension around the back of the boat on the Moth and F101 or through the middle on the Waszp, maintaining the tiller position at maximum turn (note that you generally have elastic on the boat to centralise the tiller if you let go, so ensure that you push hard against it at all times to ensure the bow goes all the way through the wind).

- As the tiller extension hits the wing on the other side, tap it down and maintain slight pressure to ensure the tiller continues to turn the boat: centralising at this stage will kill the turn and end up with the boat head to wind. This should be a flowing movement of push, swing, tap, pressure, open hand.
- With an open hand you can slide it up the tiller extension as you move the feet and body through the boat so that you end up through the wind, the new leeward wing in the water in the secure (Meerkat) position but steering behind your back. **Make sure that your old back foot moves forwards as you cross the boat, if you don't you will pivot around the back foot and you will end up sitting too far back in the boat.**
- During this period the front mainsheet hand will have grasped the mainsheet falls as you passed through the boat on the Moth and F101 (the Wasp does not have this). This helps with stability and puts you in a good position as you build on your skill set and advance into foiling transitions. With your hands in their pre-tack position you can firmly flick the battens being attentive to the power coming on as you do so. To do this on the Waszp you will need to pull sharply on the mainsheet.
- Once you are stable on the new tack you should 'swap hands' by taking the pre-tack mainsheet hand back to take the tiller in either a pan handle grip or a dagger grip.
- Either method will leave the old tiller hand free to move from steering behind your back and to take the mainsheet by picking up the mainsheet with the little finger closest to the block.
- The tiller should then be brought in front of you so that you can once again steer and sheet at the same time.

The low-riding tack on the water

This is perhaps one of the most difficult skills to teach sailors who have developed their own tacking techniques in the various classes they have sailed all their lives. Some will want to face backwards, some to let go of the tiller and or mainsheet completely but the importance of this cannot be overstated as you will need sound, accurate, repeatable skills to progress onto foiling transitions, so best learn now! There are other ways to do this but these are the best options that we tend to stick with:

- If you chose pan handle grip, use the finger walk over method to achieve this.
- If you chose dagger grip and if your tiller extension is short enough, simply pull it through the gap at your armpit being careful not to snag it on baggy clothing.

At this stage, you will be confident in at least having a good idea of how to turn around: so you should be able to get back to where you started.

KEY POINTS

1 Do not attempt to tack unless you are low riding, with speed on a proper close-hauled course.
2 As soon as the boat is just past head to wind, flicking the battens by using the boom and heeling the boat to windward as you change sides will help turn the boat through the wind.
3 There is no rush to swap hands. Get the boat stable in the secure position before attempting the tiller / mainsheet swap.
4 Keep pushing the tiller through the tack against the elastic. If the tiller returns to a central position, the boat will end up head to wind and going backwards. This can cause damage to the wand and will likely end in a further capsize.
5 Adopting the pan handle tack is our preferred method as we find greater success when advancing on to foil gybing.

LOW-RIDING TACK TROUBLESHOOTING

Problem	Cause	Solution
Boat gets stuck in irons	Initiated the tack too far off the wind or with insufficient speed	Make sure you are sailing as fast as you can on a low riding close-hauled course. Pulling the new windward wing into the water and popping the battens will help turn the boat away from the wind on the new tack.
Boat gets stuck in irons	The leeward wing hits the water slowing it down and pulling the boat back away from the wind	Make sure the boat is rolled to windward in the tack, better to hit the old windward wing in the water.
Boat gets stuck in irons	Insufficient steering	You must push hard as the elastic will centralise the tiller and the boat will not turn. Sail off on the new tack before swapping your hands: there is no rush and steering is key!

LOW-RIDING GYBE: MOTH

Essentially, the technique for the low-riding gybe is the same as the tack in that the mechanics of the tiller and mainsheet management remain the same. If you know the tack, the gybe is pretty straightforward.

- Preparation: If the boat is in a foiling mode, the boat should be slowed and sailed in a low-riding mode. It is best to have a low-riding gybe well rehearsed so that you at least know the mechanics prior to going for a full foiling gybe.
- Once the boat is stable the manoeuvre is initiated by body weight and the boat is steered to compensate and maintain stability.
- Move the back foot into the middle of the boat (Meerkat: making sure the foot moves forwards – it is going to become the front foot). Once in the secure position maintain a stable platform (the steering, weight relationship is key).
- Pull the tiller firmly away and move body weight to maintain the boat in a horizontal plane (more often than not you will dip a wing, but try to avoid this as it will kill the boatspeed and the chances of a successful turn). If you are going to dip a wing on the gybe it is much better to dip the new windward wing as this will be a key component when moving into the foiling gybe.
- Swing the tiller extension around the back of the boat (except in the Waszp), maintaining the tiller position at maximum turn (note that you generally have elastic on the Moth to centralise the tiller if you let go, so ensure that you push hard against it to make the boat steer through the gybe).
- As the tiller extension hits the wing on the other side, tap it down and maintain slight pressure to ensure the tiller continues to turn the boat – centralising at this stage will kill the turn and end up with the boat pointing downwind. This should be a flowing movement of push, swing, tap, pressure. If you end up steering straight at this point you will not commit the weight to the new side and will end up with body weight trapped on the central hull. (We call this the prayer position in the Moth as prayer is the only possible solution if you hope to hope to avoid the inevitable capsize!)
- With an open hand you can slide it up the extension as you move the feet and body through the boat (key point on moving the old back foot forwards) so that you end up on the opposite gybe, steering behind your back.
- During this period the front mainsheet hand will have grasped the mainsheet falls as you passed through the boat (except in the Waszp). This helps with stability and puts you in a good position as you build on your skill set and advance into foiling transitions. With your hands in their pre-gybe position you can firmly flick the battens being attentive to the power coming on as you do so.
- Once you are stable you should 'swap hands' by taking the pre-gybe mainsheet hand back to take the tiller in either a pan handle grip or a dagger grip.
- Either method will leave the old tiller hand free to move from steering behind your back and to take the mainsheet by grabbing the mainsheet with the little finger closest to the block.
- The tiller should then be brought in front of you so that you can once again steer and sheet at the same time:
  - If you chose pan handle grip, use the finger walk over method to achieve this.
  - If you chose dagger grip and if your tiller extension is short enough, simply pull it through the gap at your armpit being careful not to snag it on baggy clothing.
  - The third option is to pull the tiller extension over with an underhand grip, pass it briefly to the mainsheet hand whilst you change the back hand into the more conventional dagger grip.

Low-riding gybe

DIFFERENCES FOR F101

LOW-RIDING TACK: F101

The F101 tack is essentially the same as the Moth / Waszp except that the code zero may be deployed. If this is the case it actually makes the tack a bit easier as the sail can be left cleated in and once the boat reaches head to wind it will turn the boat rapidly onto the new tack. The zero can then be un-cleated on the old side, and it will blow through to the new side where it can be re-cleated.

LOW-RIDING GYBE: F101

The F101 gybe is essentially the same as the Moth / Waszp except that the code zero may be deployed. The sail should be left cleated in and once the boat is through the wind on a broad reach on the new side the zero can be un-cleated on the old side, and it will blow through to the new side where it can be re-cleated.

Gybing the F101

Tacking the F101: backing the code zero makes this easier

Objective: To return the boat to shore.

Overview: Coming ashore is an area of sailing a foiling boat which has a few potential difficulties. These are dependent on the wind direction and water depth. As with any boat, landing on a shore with the wind running along it is easiest, with added degrees of difficulty with offshore and onshore winds. As with launching, if you do have someone to help manage your boat at these moments, it certainly makes life much easier and potentially less damaging on your boat.

MOTH LANDINGS

Just as with launching, the fixed nature of the Moth's foils adds a complication that you need to think about even before you go afloat. You have to know that you can get back to shore safely without damaging yourself or the boat. Making a mental note of a safe depth for your foils on the way out will help make sure you get out in the correct depth of water on the way back. This is key: too shallow and you risk foil damage; too deep and you will have to swim yourself AND the boat into a position where you can touch the bottom. After an exhausting sailing session this is the last thing that you will need. If sailing on a falling tide you might be left with a very long carry of your boat back to your trolley so it is worth thinking about the return journey BEFORE you go out.

CROSS-SHORE WIND

The cross-shore landing is the easiest landing as you approach on a reach. In good time make sure that you return the boat to a low-riding mode and sail with the leeward wing in the water controlling the speed until you reach your pre-planned correct depth for your exit position.

If you are confident of the depth, firstly check that you have a suitably large space to leeward that is big enough to capsize your boat into. Check also for any obstructions that may become an issue when you carry the boat on shore as you will be controlling a large object in a position where your vision is severely limited.

Simply sheet in the mainsheet hard as you turn the boat slightly into the wind and slide your feet down towards the leeward wing (making sure to stay on the outside of the traveller lines and hiking straps). Due to the wing floats, the boat should slowly capsize leaving you in the ideal position to

begin the boat lift sequence.

Tie off the mainsheet in preparation for lifting the boat and swim the boat closer to shore into a depth just before the wing starts to hit the bottom. At this point it is a reverse of the launching system.

Move your shoulders just in front of the mainsheet to find the balance point on the boom with your shoulder furthest from the boat under the boom. With the other hand you can use the upper most hiking strap to control the boat as you bend your knees, keep your back straight and lift the boat out of the water.

Keep the steps small and walk as close as you can to the wing: if you walk further away the rig tip may lift out of the water too far and we need to avoid the boat righting itself and breaking your foils. The rig tip MUST be kept downwind of the boat to ensure the wind does not lift the rig. The ability to walk in all directions to avoid obstructions whilst keeping the rig downwind of the hull is essential.

Moth coming into land

Lifting the Moth ashore

OFFSHORE WIND

The offshore wind is very much the same as cross-shore. The main difference being that you will approach the shore close-hauled, at an angle rather than at right angles. Again, in good time make sure that you return the boat to a low-riding mode and sail with the leeward wing in the water to control the speed until you reach your pre-planned correct depth for your exit position where you capsize the boat. The boat will lie with the mast tip downwind, pointing offshore from the beach, so whilst the sequence is the same as the cross-shore wind you will end up walking side step and with very little idea of what you may be walking in to.

ONSHORE WIND

Returning to shore in an onshore wind is, in some instances, the most challenging as the water conditions will be the roughest and low riding a Moth on a run does have its challenges. As long as you approach the beach on a deep broad reach at an angle to the shore rather than at right angles then a lot of the issues can be eliminated. The

closer to a beam reach the better as the boat will be easier to sail and you will have to do less of a turn as you capsize the boat at the pre-selected point. The difficulty now is that you have to ensure the mast tip (pointing towards the shore) stays out of the ground as you have to cope with carrying the boat uphill, all whilst walking sideways.

With all of the landings, it is imperative to leave your boat safely in a position where it cannot damage other people or itself. It is good practice to remove the foils and return the boat onto its launching trolley as soon as possible. An unpredicted windshift or gust could be expensive.

The Moth recovery is the reverse of the launching sequence. Firstly, put the foil covers on the horizontals, remove the main foil and stow the wand, place the trolley on the boat and fasten it securely. Remove the rudder, being aware that the boat may fall forwards onto the trolley so anticipate this and control the roll forwards. Finally, release the knot from the mainsheet and roll the boat back up onto the wheels of the trolley. Remove the rig.

F101 LANDINGS

The F101's retractable foils and main halyard make it easier to land than a Moth, but it can still be a tricky manoeuvre which requires thinking about.

CROSS-SHORE WIND

The cross-shore landing is probably the easiest to execute in terms of controlling the speed and direction of the approach. The key to the success is planning in advance where you are going to land, depowering the sails and preparing to lift the foils so the boat can operate in the shallower water. Make sure you stow the code zero first. To balance the boat you will need to pull the windward hull into the water on top of you. The boat will have a tendency to bear away at this stage but, if you push the tiller away, the boat will sit quite happily in a sort of hove-to position where you can start to release the foils from their locked down position.

Release the main foil / daggerboard first. Undo the hold down line from the cleat and attach the

up elastic that is found on the front of the mast. Moving the ride height adjuster at this stage to the green side will minimise any stress on the wand. This should hold the foil in a half up position which will give you enough control to sail the boat but enough foil out of the water so that you can get out of the boat and stand on the bottom in waist depth water.

At this stage you can go to the back of the boat and release the rudder pin. Set the downhaul line to a suitable depth (you can put knots in this line at pre-set depths that will suit your regular sailing venue). As the boat moves forwards, the rudder has a natural tendency to lift until it hits the stop knot in the cleat. Make sure that you leave enough

Raising the main foil

Raising the rudder foil

rudder down to maintain steerage as you make your final approach.

Now sail in slowly and, when you reach your pre-determined stopping position, push the tiller away and sheet the mainsail in and slide off the windward hull. Remember: do not pass head to wind as the boom will hit the main foil / daggerboard when you are sailing in shallow water. Hold the boat just off head to wind whilst you recover the boat onto the trolley.

This is the bit where you can ask whether any boat is truly a single-hander. The Moth is as you can carry it out the water by yourself, park it and then go and find your trolley: most craft that have a launching trolley will require help to recover the boat as, at a minimum, you will need to get the trolley to the boat and you can't be in two places at one time.

When putting the F101 onto its trolley, make sure that the main foil is fully up and the rudder foil is securely in the fully up position. With one person on the bow, the other on the windward hull the boat can be pulled into position and the boat, weighing around 75kg all up, should be fairly straightforward to pull out of the water. The mainsail should be dropped or at least released from the clew to enable easier handling around the dinghy park / shore.

OFFSHORE WIND

Landing the F101 in an offshore wind basically relies on planning an approach which takes into account the final point of sail to be close-hauled when you are experiencing a lot more leeway due to the foils being half up. Sitting well forwards and keeping the bow in will help with leeway.

Set up your foil lift point upwind and, if possible, well to one side of the proposed landing spot. Lift the foils as described above and slide sideways and upwind into a depth where you can slide out of the boat and into a suitable depth of water. Care must be taken not to tack the boat with the foils up as the boom will hit against the main foil. If in any doubt, lift the foils up to a point where the boom can still pass over the foil and plan on getting out of the boat into much deeper water.

Again if you are sailing two-up, or have some help on shore ready to help with the landing, then your life will be much easier. Recover the boat in the same way as above.

Recovering the F101 onto the trolley

ONSHORE WIND

Landing the F101 in an onshore wind can best be achieved by dropping the mainsail and using the code zero to sail into the beach.

Firstly, choose your spot to take down your mainsail. The code zero should be furled and the boat lying on a reach with the windward hull in the water, tiller pushed all the way to leeward as in the hove-to position. Release the halyard and drop the mainsail, taking care to secure the sail from blowing away by using the mainsheet.

Secure the foils in an up position as previously described. Pull out some of the code zero to give you sufficient speed to execute a controlled downwind sail to your landing spot. Furl the sail as you get close and slide out of the boat to windward as you steer the boat into the wind and any waves that may be present.

Depending on the sea state, launching ramp and whether you have help, you can either recover the boat stern first by walking the trolley deeper into the water or recover in the normal way, turning the bow towards the shore and sliding the boat onto the trolley, which would be the preferred method unless the sea state would not allow it.

WASZP LANDINGS

The Waszp can come ashore following either the Moth or the F101 approach.

1 To lower the mainsail at sea, with the windward hull in the water on a reach, release the main halyard

2 Pull the mainsail down

3...and pull

4...and pull

Sailing the F101 downwind with just the code zero

Objective: To get the boat upright from a capsized position.

Overview: Recovering your boat from a capsize is the most exhausting of exercises whilst learning and can put a premature end to your day of foiling. The ability to get into your boat without damaging it and, more importantly, yourself is paramount.

CAPSIZING

Something that we should talk about prior to the capsize recovery are the actual skills required to capsize safely! It is really easy to break things when capsizing as you can introduce loads onto the boat and its parts at angles that the designer had never thought about. A few basics will save costly repairs to your boat as well as less risk of personal injury. There are generally 3 ways to capsize your boat and we will deal with each of them in turn.

Windward capsize

WINDWARD CAPSIZE

This is possibly the capsize which will likely cause the least damage. When falling in to windward the sailor will get swept aft and have a disconnect to the hiking straps. The main key here is to let go of the tiller: keep hold of the mainsheet by all means, but gripping the tiller extension as you depart the boat backwards will break it, the tiller or transom of the boat. Hang on to the mainsheet if you must but I say again: let go of the tiller at all costs!

LEEWARD CAPSIZE

There are two possible versions of this capsize. The one you want to avoid is where you capsize to leeward and fall backwards over the high side of the boat where the main foil will be waiting: avoid this at all costs as there is potential for serious injury. Make sure you fall inside the boat.

The second version of this is the standard and 'BEST' leeward capsize where you fall down inside the boat. The key here is to recognise that you are sailing a Moth: you are going to get wet, so do not hold on to the windward wing and gently lower yourself down because the boat will turn turtle really quickly and you will still end up wet AND with the boat inverted.

The best option here is to recognise the capsize early and plan your landing area which should ideally be behind the mainsheet as you avoid entanglement. Make sure that you get your feet outside the hiking straps as these can also be a source of entrapment. Also, do not be tempted to jump (or even step) on the mast, boom or sail – serious expense will follow. Plan your drop, and accept that you are going to get wet! Generally, attempts to dry capsize end badly.

Leeward capsize

PITCHPOLE

The pitchpole is a fairly common end to what had been, up until that point, a pleasant foil. It is the capsize with the most potential of hitting something either solid or expensive, so it can be high tariff!

The pitchpole can be caused by the main foil coming out of the water so, as well as it having the potential for high speed, it may also be from altitude so, as the bow goes down, there is little volume in the bow to push it out: it eventually comes to a stop and you will be thrown forwards. Generally, if you are hiking out then you will miss the shrouds and lowers and you can make a dive forwards and to windward so will have a relatively soft water landing.

Pitchpole

The issues may come if you are not hiking out HARD, or because you are in the middle of a tack or gybe. Either way, being thrown forwards at speed into the boat will always hurt so wearing a helmet, buoyancy aid and a few milimetres of neoprene will help ease the pain of any potential contact. The best advice is always hike out and stay out from the area between the shrouds as much as you can.

MOTH CAPSIZE RECOVERY

There are two methods of recovering from a capsize in the Moth (including the Waszp):
- The leg-over
- The waterstart

We will describe each here, but the leg-over is our preferred method for beginners, and we only resort to the waterstart when the first approach does not work as intended.

THE LEG-OVER

The leg-over is the technique we described when launching the Moth (p43), and the capsize recovery follows exactly the same approach.

Before starting to bring the boat upright: prepare.

From inside the boat, make sure the mainsheet is untangled with the end looped over the hiking strap and the tiller extension is resting on top of the sail above the boom, then proceed as on p44.

THE WATERSTART

Sometimes when we are learning, the timing of the leg-over may not be perfect or we may have fallen out of the boat. Being able to waterstart MAY save the day and quite a lot of energy. However, it has a high failure rate when you are learning and it can often be less time and energy consuming simply to let the boat capsize and start again.

Generally, the boat will be heeled to windward. In this state it will have a tendency to want to bear away from the wind where it will invariably capsize to windward leaving the boom in the air. This will result in a complete turtle and a few minutes of boat wrestling to get it back in position from which you can attempt the more attainable leg-over.

IF you can get the boat positioned on a beam reach or closer to the wind and your back hand on the tiller extension pushing as far as you can to keep the boat pointing more upwind, then you have a good chance of completing a waterstart.

With the wing flush to the water reach in for the toestrap, sliding your body over the wing so that your front hand can pull you head first into the boat so that you can grab the falls of the mainsheet. This will enable you to pull in the sail (to windward and past the middle of the boat if necessary), to slowly push the leeward wing into the water. You can now regain the secure (Meerkat) position.

KEY POINTS

1 When learning the capsize, default to the leg-over: it is more reliable. Attempting the waterstart is rarely effective for the beginner.

2 If you re-capsize the boat to leeward (i.e. the boat blows straight over when you reach in for the tiller), start again but pull the windward wing into the water to counteract the windage in the rig. This only works in 10 knots or more of wind. Once the boat is steered into the beam reach position it is always best to replace the leeward wing against the water in preparation to get in to the secure position ready for sailing.

3 In lighter winds having the boat heeled on top of you to windward will leave you in a very uncomfortable body position, unable to steer and unable to fully pull the mainsheet in. Getting the leeward wing on top of the water is essential.

1 With the wing flush to the water reach for the toestrap

2 Pull yourself into the boat

3 Climb onboard

4 And regain the secure position

CAPSIZE TROUBLESHOOTING

Problem	Cause	Solution
I can't get my leg over / I am too short	Getting in the boat too early	Wait for the boat to start coming up, make sure you roll towards the front of the boat and don't climb in with an upright body.
I am not strong / heavy enough	Too much windage / lightweight	Use the main foil vertical as a lever by stepping back to free water from the sail; fit some righting lines.
Boat capsizes again before I am in	Getting in the boat too early	Get into the boat later.
Boat capsizes when I go to reach for the tiller or mainsheet	Water is still covering trampoline or tiller / mainsheet is to leeward	Keep your weight to windward until water is displaced from the trampoline. Make sure you set up the tiller on the boom and mainsheet over the hiking strap prior to righting the boat. If it is windy you might even think of dipping the windward wing into the water before reaching for the tiller and mainsheet.

F101 CAPSIZE RECOVERY

It has to be said that if you have capsized the F101 then you have been trying extremely hard! The boat has been designed with a wide base and low rig in order to minimise capsize potential. However, if you should capsize the boat (and it is not impossible), it will inevitably turn turtle quite quickly. This is how you right it:

- Get on the rear of one float and sink the corner so the boat rights to the capsize position.
- Now put your weight on the main foil to pull the boat upright.
- As with any multihull, if the wind gets under the sail, it will come upright quite quickly.
- As the boat comes upright, move to the front beam and enter the boat by sliding over the beam. Once you have rested, prepare the boat for sailing again.

The F101 will usually turn turtle if you capsize

1 Weigh down one float

2 Climb onto the float

3 Pull down on the main foil

4 Keep your weight on the foil

5 Let the boat come up

6 And up

7 Till it rests on the leeward float

8 Then climb in over the mainbeam staying outside of the shroud and compression strut

PART 3
FLYING

FIRST FLIGHT

Objective: Move the boat from a low-riding, stable, beam reaching position up onto a fully foiling reach for the first time.

Overview: As the boat speed increases, the apparent wind will move forwards. At this stage you should steer the boat a little further off the wind on a beam reach into the take-off zone on the diagram (trimmed to the apparent wind) so you avoid having to sail with the rig trimmed for close-hauled sailing.

This will enable a little more margin for error on the trimming because, once the boat lifts up on the foils, it is going to accelerate and swing the apparent wind even further forwards. This means that, if you have no way of trimming in further to stop the sail back winding and / or de-powering, you will have to quickly steer the boat away from the wind which, when you are foiling for the first time, can be another variable we would try to avoid having. If you end up block-to-block on the mainsheet you will run into your own apparent wind and the boat will fall in to windward so you will need to steer to a goal point further off the wind.

Assuming that you have set the boat up correctly there are 3 variables that we need to control:

1. Righting moment. We take out this variable by sitting still and NO hiking out initially.
2. Steering. We take out this variable by steering in a straight line heading for a goal point on a beam reach course.
3. Trimming. This is what we will focus on. You will trim for 'balance', pulling in and easing the sail to keep the boat sailing as fast as you can whilst ensuring the boat is perfectly 'flat' or slightly heeled to windward.

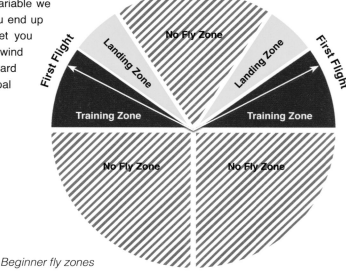

Beginner fly zones

GETTING UP ON THE FOILS

In terms of getting up on the foils, the key points are:

- Do not hike, no body movements. It is tempting to move your body, but don't!
- Your body should generally be still, sat in the middle of the wing bar with the boat trimmed flat fore and aft, the back foot under the hiking strap.
- Maintain a steady course, keeping your head out of the boat and your boat steering towards a chosen goal point as indicated in the diagram. Many beginners will get wind blindness and lose orientation of wind direction. A visual goal point is essential.
- Keep the boat balanced by trimming the sail. As the speed increases, make sure that the boat is at least upright. Heeling the boat slightly to windward, on top of you, is the aim. This will feel alien and uncomfortable but get used to it fast. ANY heeling to leeward will stall the foil and will prevent the boat taking off.
- The boat should be trimmed flat fore and aft, the take-off should be level and NOT bow up as you might expect. This is because we have set the boat up with the correct angles of attack on both the main foil AND the rudder foil and we want a smooth take-off, not a leap out of the water.
- We will say this again: the boat should be upright at worse, slightly heeled to windward at best. It should be noted that upright is a misconception in many dinghy sailors' minds and heeled to windward will feel extremely uncomfortable for many to begin with. Don't worry, you get used to it – and the rewards are incredible.

With the boat now building up speed (around 7-8 knots depending on your boat and if it is set up correctly) it will slowly begin to lift out of the water. If the fore and aft trim is correct, and the foil balance set up correctly, it should come out of the water flat and smooth. As this happens the drag from the hull is released and the boat accelerates. As the speed

My daughters enjoying their first flight

increases the apparent wind moves forwards and the sail will need to be trimmed in quickly to keep the boat powered up. Again, if you reach the block-to-block position you will need to turn further off the wind to give yourself some margin for error. At this moment you will be fully foiling and the boat will accelerate, the world will become silent and sailing will never be the same.

The next thing that will become apparent is that the steering of the boat becomes extremely sensitive. On your first flight it is good to be prepared for this as you will also experience what happens when you over steer. The best way to think about this is to consider the steering sensation to be very similar to a bicycle. If you are going fast and turn the handlebars quickly, the bike will trip up and throw you off. The Moth is similar, in that it is very sensitive to heel and rudder movements, so steering, sheeting and body movements need to be subtle. When you are learning it is better to try to isolate these areas. When learning focus initially on trimming ONLY. As you improve you will feed more subtle movements into your steering and bodyweight to ensure you maintain a stable foiling position in a much more efficient style.

Moth going up onto the foils

COMMON PROBLEMS

1. The boat will not foil

Any heel to leeward will make the horizontal foil stall. The boat MUST be at a minimum flat but preferably heeled to windward by a 5-degree angle. Bring the boat on top of you and she will lift clear of the water.

If you are heeled to leeward, the foil stalls and you will not take off

2. The boat accelerates on to the foils and very quickly falls into windward

The boat has run into the apparent wind, you must sheet in quickly and, if you have gone block-to-block, you must steer the boat further away from the wind to maintain the perfect sail trim. Be careful not to lose sight of your goal point and ensure that you do not sail too far off the wind.

If you are quickly falling into windward you have run into the apparent wind

3. The boat trips up and falls into leeward

You must keep the boat on top of you. As soon as you heel to leeward the foils will stall. Concentrate on your goal point to ensure that you are not too far off the wind and anticipate the heel by easing the mainsheet before the boat heels. As you improve a small body movement and / or a slight steering adjustment will also do the trick but focus initially on the trimming.

If you are tripping up and falling in to leeward, the foils stall: keep the boat on top of you

4. The sheet is block-to-block and you are heeling further to windward

Steer further away from the wind as you have run into your apparent wind and need to bear away in order to maintain efficient sail trim.

If you are sheeted block-to-block and heeling further to windward, bear away to increase power

HOW TO RETURN TO LOW RIDING

The time has come to turn around. The foiling novice transition should initially be the tack as described on p61. To return to low riding, and a stable platform, gently steer the boat closer to the wind into the landing zone in the diagram and allow the boat to heel to leeward by slightly over sheeting the sail or leaning in a little.

As the boat slows, and the foils stall, the apparent wind will return to the true wind so continually steer the boat slowly up into the wind

until it is low riding on a proper close-hauled course. After foiling you will be surprised how far that is away from the angle that you were foiling at but, if you do not sail a proper true wind close-hauled course, the boat will not be able to make it through the tack as the angle will be too great and you will be left stuck head to wind and going backwards. This is why the wand preventer line should be used when learning as going backwards can damage the push rods.

DIFFERENCES WITH THE F101

The F101 has no added complications in comparison to the Moth. It has the big advantage that you will not go for a swim should you get anything wrong, so the learning curve is incomparable.

The angle of the wings / floats on the F101 is pre-set so that when the windward hull is touching the water the foils are at the perfect angle to initiate foiling.

As soon as you lift the windward float clear of the water, the drag will decrease significantly and the foils will be at the correct angle ready for lift off.

Returning to a low-riding mode is the same as for the Moth. Once you are proficient you can slide the boat off the foils without touching the leeward float in the water but, if you do that initially, it is nothing to worry about, it will just slow you up a little.

F101 going up on the foils

Objective: To fly the boat upwind and downwind.

Overview: During the first few flights the tendency is that the novice foiler will sail upwind. This is partly due to a close-hauled sailing angle being more stable initially and also because we teach the tack before the gybe, as again there are greater chances of success without energy-sapping capsizes. Once you have the boat foiling there are now subtle differences in how you sail the boat more efficiently upwind and downwind.

UPWIND

To sail the boat more efficiently upwind it is essential that the boat is foiling comfortably on a reach. At this stage the boat can be steered closer to the wind but it is crucial that the boat is heeled further to windward. This will counteract the greater leeway that is produced when sailing upwind and help to give further lift from the foils pulling the boat to windward. You will now be hiking hard and using your bodyweight as your confidence and skill level increase.

Moth foiling upwind

BODY POSITION

Just behind mainsheet, fully hiked, rig pulled on top of you, boat heeling to windward.

RIG SET UP

Flat, bladed rig required so outhaul on, lots of kicking strap (vang) to close the leech and downhaul hard on for a fine entry.

BOAT SET UP

Ride height as high as you can to ensure the leeward wing tip on the main foil does not break out into the air. This is adjusted in slightly different ways on all the boats so check the manual for your own craft. (The more you improve, the higher you can fly but be careful as the margin for error becomes less.) Fore and aft trim should be slightly bow down: this is adjusted by winding more lift onto the rudder.

SAILING TECHNIQUE

Hike as hard as you can. The mainsheet should be tight in and small adjustments of bodyweight used to keep the boat sailing as fast as possible as you sail on the luff telltales (if they are not stuck to the sail!). Whilst you need a lot of mainsheet tension for sailing upwind you will find that the last few inches are the most important in terms of power.

What you will also find is that you will require a better understanding of fine steering to help control the power: remember that once you are block-to-block on the mainsheet the only way to save yourself when falling in to windward is to steer the boat further away from the wind and / or reduce your hiking.

DIFFERENCES WITH THE F101

The F101 works very much the same as the Moth and Waszp in broad terms. However, it does have a code zero which will require some differing techniques for sailing upwind and downwind and this will also depend on the wind strength.

Assuming lighter winds (under 8 knots), in general the code zero needs to be sheeted in hard and the boat initially sailed quite close to the wind. The F101 is easier to learn to foil in many respects, one of them being that the telltales on the zero give a really good indication of wind direction and what is happening in terms of apparent wind.

Using the telltales as a guide, steer the boat to sail with the zero sheeted relatively hard in and with the boat heeled over onto the windward float. You should control the power in the mainsail to balance the boat only: don't worry if it backwinds the sail to stop the boat heeling, just trim to keep the boat balanced.

As the speed increases, and the boat foils, just follow the telltales and sheet the mainsail hard in: the acceleration and the apparent wind swinging forwards will be quite sudden.

As the wind increases to 10-12 knots it is unlikely that you will be using the code zero to get upwind.

F101 foiling upwind

FOILING UPWIND TROUBLESHOOTING

Problem	Cause	Solution
Boat crashes suddenly in to windward	Stalled rig	Flatten off the sail with more vang and downhaul. Sheet hard and steer the boat further away from the wind. Move your bodyweight in if required. You will find that a quick, timely tweak of the tiller to windward may also throw the boat upright very much like the centrifugal force experienced on a bicycle.
Boat falls in to leeward	Too much power / not enough righting moment	Flatten off the rig. Sail the boat from on top of you to flat and react BEFORE the boat goes beyond upright. Sailing the boat heeled to windward will be extremely unnatural for most sailors initially.
Boat falls off the foils	Not enough speed	Sail the boat fast, sailing too close to the wind and not heeling to windward will cause the foils to stall and the boat to drop back to low riding.
Windward wing / hull keeps hitting the water	Not enough ride height when the boat is heeling to windward	Raise the ride height which will enable you to sail the boat heeled to windward.

REACHING

As soon as you become competent at foiling you generally learn that a reach is the best place to get onto the foils, but that the most fun is to be had going upwind or downwind and the reach gets overlooked. For those times when a reach is necessary, the set-up is pretty much what was taught on your first flight except that you may be hiking and using your bodyweight to greater effect.

BODY POSITION
Just behind mainsheet but NOT fully hiked. With less leeway the boat can be sailed more upright but certainly not heeled to leeward. Small body movements will be necessary to help steer the boat.

RIG SET-UP
More powerful, so kicking strap (vang), downhaul and outhaul eased slightly in comparison to the close-hauled set up.

BOAT SET-UP
On a reach the boat should be set up flat with a ride height that will be dependent on wave / chop height. If you are in doubt or feel slightly out of control you should keep the bow trimmed down by winding more lift onto the rudder. Whilst this is not fast, as there is more drag, it will give you confidence as you compress the wand and the boat feels less likely to fly out of the water.

The reach in steady winds and flat water is a good point of sailing to experiment with foil set up changes and we will deal with the fundamentals of these on p98.

SAILING TECHNIQUE
On a reach the boat should be flatter in terms of both heel and trim. As the apparent wind will move forward and aft as the wind and boat speed varies, this point of sailing will require a subtle approach in

Moth foiling on reach

combining the effects of sail trim, body movement and steering. As your ability to control the boat with a controlled combination of adjustments improves you can really start to use the reach as a 'training run' before you are finally ready to send the boat on a more downwind angle.

DIFFERENCES WITH THE F101
In lighter winds the F101 may deploy the code zero to get up on the foils. Sailing technique for this would be to sheet the sail in quite hard and then use the mainsail trimming only as a method of balancing the boat, the main propulsion being taken care of by the zero. The boat will be very stable on this point of sail with this configuration but as speeds increase you may well end up sailing on a broad reach as the apparent wind comes so far forward.

FOILING ON A REACH TROUBLESHOOTING

Problem	Cause	Solution
Boat takes off and out of the water and pitchpoles forwards	Too much flap / ride height / angle of attack on main foil and / or insufficient rudder lift	Move forwards, compress the wand and lower your ride height. Increase lift on the rudder.

DOWNWIND SAILING

This is probably the most difficult point of sailing to attain when you are learning to foil. The issue is the concept of apparent wind, which is very much exaggerated when sailing deep downwind while foiling as the sail will be sheeted as if you are sailing upwind. This is when many sailors lose all bearing of wind direction and suffer from what we term 'wind blindness'.

Visual clues, such as telltales, are not normally helpful as they are often wet and stuck to the sail, burgees / wind indicators will be swept off during capsizes and crashes, so the only reasonable tool you can use is a streamer on the forestay but even this is often found stuck or wrapped around the wire.

This results in a reliance upon a 'feel' which has yet to be experienced / learned or a visual transit on the land. Either way, it is important to maintain an awareness of the true wind angle. As you improve with your downwind sailing you will find that the downwind no-fly zone becomes narrower.

BODY POSITION

Just behind mainsheet but NOT fully hiked. The body should come more upright into a sitting rather than a hiking position as the boat needs to come into an upright position. As in the reaching position, small body movements will be necessary to help balance the boat as it is steered onto a run.

Whilst it may be counterintuitive to the dinghy sailor, who will naturally feel compelled to move backwards as they go downwind, it is actually better to move the weight forward, compress the wand, drive the bow down and keep the main foil in the water. If you see the bow in the air and the wand flicking forwards then it is likely that the main foil will be coming out of the water shortly and you should prepare for a pitchpole.

RIG SET-UP

Very much like the reaching set-up: the kicking strap (vang), downhaul and outhaul should be eased to offer maximum power.

BOAT SET-UP

Again, like the reach, the boat should be set up flat with a ride height that will be dependent on wave / chop height. On a run the boat is more likely to pop the main foil out of the water as you are now finding the boat more or less in alignment with the wind produced wave peaks and troughs. This is where, if you have the boat riding too high with the bow up, you can see a big pothole in the water in front of you and the main foil can come out of the water causing the boat to crash bow first.

If you are in doubt, or feel slightly out of control, you should keep the bow trimmed down by winding more lift on to the rudder and setting the boat to ride lower in the water. This does, of course, cause more drag but it will give you confidence which, at this stage, is the key to getting downwind successfully.

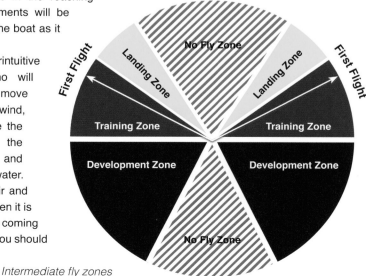

Intermediate fly zones

SAILING TECHNIQUE

To initiate the downwind turn the boat should be foiling fast on an angle at least 90-100 degrees off the true wind with the sail sheeted just off the centreline. The boat, which will be slightly heeled to windward at this point, should be brought upright. This is achieved by subtle movements of body and tiller and, as the boat is sent confidently on to a very broad reach direction, you will find the boat accelerates rapidly.

To keep up with the acceleration and the associated forward movement of the apparent wind, the sail should be eased and trimmed appropriately to ensure that the sail does not stall. IF the flow does unattach itself at this speed it can result in the boat falling to windward. This can be saved by steering the boat back upwind (which will have the effect of bringing the boat upright) and trimming the sail. By employing these techniques, the flow on the sail can be reattached and the whole process repeated.

When you are first trying this, the rudder / sail trim / body movements are exaggerated and a little agricultural. As you improve the previous wild 'S' shapes that you have been carving in the water with the foils will even out into much more gentle curves.

Moth foiling downwind

F101 foiling downwind

DIFFERENCES WITH THE F101

The F101 can be sailed in exactly the same way as the Moth downwind. However, having the code zero will help the boat sail deeper angles than it would be able to achieve under the mainsail alone.

FOILING DOWNWIND TROUBLESHOOTING

Problem	Cause	Solution
Boat takes off and out of the water and pitchpoles forwards	Too much flap / ride height / angle of attack on main foil and / or insufficient rudder lift	Move forwards, compress the wand and lower your ride height. Put more lift on the rudder.
You can't bear off onto a run	The boat is heeled to leeward, the boat is not powered up and going fast	Commit to the bear away, heel the boat on top of you, sheeting hard as you accelerate downwind.

Objective: To stay on the foils all the way through the transition.

Overview: Initially, the foiling gybe should be the focus of the novice foiler. The foiling tack is much more difficult and is only likely to be successful once all of the basic skills have been achieved consistently to a very high level.

THE FOILING GYBE

The foiling gybe itself is viewed as the initial holy grail for the improving foiler and the temptation to attempt this before you are ready is generally too great for most mortals to resist. The reality is that, to achieve a foiling gybe, you must first be a competent foiling sailor who is confident sailing on a run with an extremely narrow downwind no-fly zone as shown in the diagram.

REMEMBER: The foiling gybe can only be achieved when the fundamental techniques of foiling have been mastered. As your general sailing gets better and better so do the chances of completing your very first fully foiling gybe.

At Pro-Vela we developed the following sequence to describe the phases of the successful foiling gybe.

THE SIX S'S OF THE FOILING GYBE

1. Speed
The first priority for a foiling gybe is speed into the turn.

The gybe will consist of turning the boat downwind from one 'tack' to the other with the boom crossing

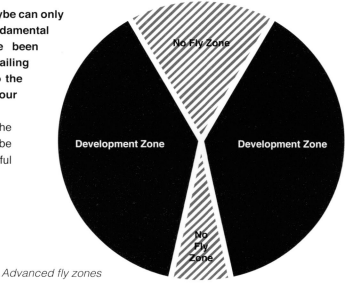

Advanced fly zones

the centreline of the boat. The faster you are going, the further forward the apparent wind will be, so the smaller the gybing arc will need to be. The slower you are going, the further the boat will need to turn which will result in more speed being lost and, ultimately, the boat falling off the foils. Speed is your friend and the temptation to slow down for the turn must be resisted at all costs. Sailing flat out with the sail sheeted near the centreline on the apparent wind is the ideal set-up.

2. Stability

I often watch people going 'quite' fast in their boats. You watch the really good sailors going fast and you see the difference in how effortless the good sailor seems to make everything look. The novice is going fast but their movements are agricultural: too much rudder means too much compensation on bodyweight and / or sheet trimming and the result is a wild west bucking bronco show which you know is going to end up with the cowboy being thrown off!

With such small margins for error in all of the 3 major variables that we discussed earlier (weight, trimming and steering), the sailor ends up chasing each error by over correcting on another variable. We always try to cut down these variables initially by getting sailors to sit still, no body movement, and to steer in a straight line to a given goal point – the only variable being the trimming.

As you improve it is easier to pick a new goal point and again trim the boat flat by using sheet trim only: the bodyweight should only be used as a last resort as it is also the least effective method to control the boat. Once the sailor is capable of foiling on all points of sailing and is comfortably in control on a very broad reach then you are ready to attempt the next stage.

3. Shift Weight

It is really important to initiate a foiling gybe by shifting the body weight BEFORE you steer.

As the rear foot comes out of the hiking strap, the sailor slides the foot to the middle of the boat and rises up on the front knee, maintaining a position we commonly call the Meerkat, or Secure Position. This action will commit the weight on the

inside of the turn, slightly banking the boat towards the centre of the turn. This concept is absolutely imperative to the success of the gybe.

For anyone who has ever ridden a bicycle or a scooter (and that is most of us), you will know that if you turn the handlebars before you lean into the turn then you fall off on the outside of the turn. Most initial failures of gybes can be put down to either lack of speed and stability OR no commitment of weight to the inside of the turn.

At this stage the tiller is rotated around the back of the boom and placed firmly onto the new wing and the hand is palm down and open which will allow the sailor to slide the hand over the extension whilst maintaining slight downward pressure as they move swiftly across the boat.

The sheet hand at this time grips the mainsheet with a V between the thumb and index finger and reaches for the cascade of mainsheet and grasps the falls between the boom and mainsheet blocks. As the body moves through to the other side of the boat you will have to duck under the boom (which is still on the old gybe and hopefully sheeted near the centreline) and go straight into a Meerkat (secure position) on the new gybe. You will have seen many photos of this position where the sailor is through the gybe on the new tack before the boom has moved onto the new leeward side.

As was mentioned earlier, most failures end with the boat falling on the outside of the turn. Have the aim that, if you are going to fall over, make sure that you fall on the inside of the turn. (The upside of this is that, if you do not foil all the way through, you will at least be able to recover, sail off and give it another try.)

4. Steer

At this stage the boat is gently steered into the turn – at these kinds of speeds you have to remember that a little rudder goes a long way – and again, very much like your bicycle, it is imperative to bank the boat ever so slightly into the inside of the turn.

As your body previously slid under the boom and pivoted forwards onto the new side of the boat, the tiller is now controlled with your hand behind your back. It is here that your previously developed skills

Moth doing a foiling gybe

of using steering to balance the boat really pay off as the small changes in bodyweight and steering maintain the boat's speed and stability through the gybe. (Steering with your hand behind your back is an essential skill which improves with practice and confidence.)

You can now help the sail onto the new side by flicking the sail battens. This is achieved by pumping the mainsheet falls as the boat is steered through to a broad reach on the new tack whilst still continuing to sail with the mainsheet and tiller in the old hands.

The timing of the shifting of weight and steering is key to the success of the gybe. You MUST commit to the inside of the turn and fully move your body onto the new gybe much earlier than you think possible. You will be on the new side before the boom has crossed over onto the new side. Steering will have a huge influence on your ability to maintain the balance of the boat throughout the turn. You should come out of the gybe on the new side steering with your hand behind your back and with the mainsheet in your wrong (back) hand.

5. Swap Hands

ONLY when the boat is back sailing in a stable fashion on the new side should the hand swap be attempted. There is absolutely no rush to complete

Waszp doing a foiling gybe

this phase of the gybe and many a good gybe has finished in a wet ending due to a rushed hand swap caused by the excitement of getting 'through' the gybe on the foils. The hand swap is exactly the same technique that has been previously learned in your basic turning drills. You knew there must have been a reason for doing that!

6. Smile

When you are still on the foils hiking on the new tack with your hands back in their sailing positions then you can allow yourself a smile.

DIFFERENCES WITH THE WASZP

The technique for the Waszp is basically the same as the Moth but the tiller extension will need to be passed through the middle of the boat. This does not cause any unexpected problems and in fact many people who have sailed Lasers will be very much used to this technique anyway. The Waszp does not have mainsheet falls so your technique will be slightly different in that you will need to rely on the battens flicking themselves as you get pressure into the new side of the sail.

Moth sailors converting to the Waszp find this more difficult but, as with most things, you just need to repeat the movement enough times until the muscle memory starts to work and you can rely on the kinesthesis rather than thinking or even looking at what you are doing instead of getting your head out of the boat. This is why the learning of these techniques from the start is so important and why we put so much emphasis into the tiller and mainsheet drills.

DIFFERENCES WITH THE F101

The F101 has the ability to use both the round the back (Moth) AND the through the middle (Waszp) tiller extension techniques: the sailor can choose, but it is far better to choose one technique and stick to it.

Doing a foiling gybe in the F101 is more challenging with the code zero flying – if it backs at all it will bring the boat off the foils, so you need to have a way of gybing the zero as well as the mainsail.

F101 doing a foiling gybe

FOILING GYBE TROUBLESHOOTING

Problem	Cause	Solution
Boat capsizes to windward on entry	Centrifugal force 'throws' the boat to the outside of the turn very much like turning on a bicycle	Make sure that you keep the boat leaning into the centre of the turn. If you fail in a gybe when learning, make sure you fail with the inside wing in the water.
Boat porpoises on entry and gets out of control	The sailor is nervous and tentative on entry to the gybe and slows down	Drive the boat into the turn at full speed, the faster the better. Sail it like you stole it! And sheet hard as you accelerate into the turn.
Boat won't foil all the way through the turn	Not enough speed / control before entry	You are probably not ready to foil gybe. Get your skill set up. You MUST be confident in sailing your boat at high speed on a broad reach in total control before you will have success at the foiling gybe.
Boat capsizes to leeward	A nice problem to have and not so common for the beginner but caused by not enough speed or turning too slowly for the amount of bodyweight you have committed to the inside of the turn	Steering will invariably be the key to fix this. By moving the rudder you can throw the balance of the boat one way or the other to maintain stability. If you feel the leeward wing going down, just steer harder into the turn which will throw the inside wing higher.
Boat gybes but drops off the foils on the new gybe	There is nothing as frustrating as this, but you are very close to success! This is generally caused by premature tiller and mainsheet manipulation.	Don't be in a rush to swap hands. Sail out of the gybe with your 'old' hand positions. When you have stabilised the boat and you are happily on the new tack sailing THEN you can change hands.
Boat capsizes to leeward as you exit the gybe	Power surge as battens 'pop' on the new side or you have steered too quickly for the amount of weight you have on the new side	This can be hard on the Waszp as there are no mainsheet 'falls' to grab and manually pop the battens. The Moth and F101 battens can be flicked when the rig is very light due to the apparent wind being far forward so the power comes on earlier and more gradually. Steering to the power that you have to maintain stability is the key skill to acquire.

THE FOILING TACK

The foiling tack has only really become possible as Moths became more efficient and sailors became much more proficient. With the latest foil developments glide distances have improved and this has opened a much greater possibility of the foiling tack being achieved by sailors who are less than full-time athletes.

From a coaches perspective the foiling tack is very similar in technique terms to the foiling gybe as it is all about timing and smooth movement BUT the mainsheet and tiller hand transitions are more complex and require breaking of a golden rule of sailing: that rule of never letting go of the tiller.

The preparation of the boat and body for the foiling tack is quite straightforward. Ideally in flat (preferably warm!) water, 8-10 knots of stable wind. With the boat foiling fast high and stable, the turn will again be initiated by the shifting of bodyweight.

- Bring the boat upright so that the platform is flat and not heeled to windward: this can be achieved by bearing away slightly to power up and speed up slightly.
- Slip the rear foot out of the hiking strap and roll the body upwards: this will mean that you need to depower the rig by steering into the wind, the speed at which you turn will be governed by how fast you can move across the boat.
- As you move the tiller extension around the back and lock it off by pushing down on the tiller against the wing you will be moving swiftly across the boat and you will need to ease the mainsheet as you will need to turn the boat further away from the wind than the close-hauled position.
- It is at this point, with the bodyweight through and onto at least the middle of the new trampoline on the new tack, that you will need to do the unthinkable and briefly let go of the tiller. The elastic that you have fitted across the tiller will hold it centrally so you will need the boat flat and balanced and be in full control of the mainsheet for stability as you drop the tiller and pass the mainsheet into the

new hand, all the time trimming it to the new tack and the specific angle you have chosen when you dropped your tiller.
- You can quickly pick up the tiller in the new back hand and walk it over into the dagger grip that you would normally use for upwind sailing.

The success of this will depend on excellent control of the 3 variables of steering, bodyweight and trimming and a lot of practice in order to get consistent timing. With good boat set-up and a lot of practice you will find that the foiling tack becomes attainable.

Like all sailing skills, the hard work required needs to be put in but some coaching and video feedback will be invaluable if you have access to it as it will enable you to break the skill into achievable sections:

- The same as the foiling gybe you will need to be foiling fast into the tack making sure that you have a flat, stable platform.
- Shift your body weight first and then steer to the weight making sure you move quickly and smoothly through the boat and commit fully to the new side.
- Squeeze the mainsail on as the boat comes into the wind (and then you will need a quick ease to ensure the boat pops all the way through the wind and slightly broader than your new close-hauled course (if you have the main pinned in it will prematurely power up the sail and trip the boat up).
- As the boat reaches its new angle on the new tack the sail needs to be quickly sheeted in: there is no time to perform the usual hand swap, so we need to let go of the tiller and this gives a moment of time when both hands are on the mainsheet and it can be trimmed accurately and quickly to control sail power to the required level to support the weight that you have moved through.
- Pick up the tiller in the back hand and walk over the tiller into its normal sailing position.

Moth doing a foiling tack

Timing is everything! Only by repeating and practising will you learn to perform this move consistently. Having a great boat that glides effortlessly through the tack will also give you more time and stability: you will find this much easier on the most recent generation of Moths and you will require the skills of a Ninja to get it done with older generation foils.

DIFFERENCES WITH THE WASZP AND F101

The foiling tack on the Waszp is similar in technique to the Moth except that the tiller will go forwards rather than round the back but, as you have learned this all the way through your Waszp journey, this will not come as a shock to the system. The challenge with the Waszp is that it is heavier and has less efficient foils than the Moth so the margin for error is much less.

The F101 has the same mechanics in terms of technique as the Moth but again, as a heavier boat, keeping it on the foils all the way through the tack will be challenging.

FOILING TACK TROUBLESHOOTING

Problem	Cause	Solution
Boat falls in to windward BEFORE going through the wind	Too much weight on windward side, you have either moved too late OR steered too quickly	Move the bodyweight before steering the boat into the wind. Timing is everything. Keep the boat flat.
Boat falls in to leeward BEFORE going through the wind	Too much power in the rig or not enough righting moment	Again, you have steered too late or moved your weight too early…timing is everything.
Boat falls in to windward AFTER going through the wind	Too much weight on windward side, OR not enough power in the sail	You are almost there! Sheet in harder / faster or steer a bit further through the wind.
Boat falls in to leeward AFTER going through the wind	Too much power in the rig or not enough righting moment	Again, if you have foiled through the wind you are close! Ease the sail more after the battens have flicked or move further through the boat.
Boat stalls head to wind	Poor boat set-up, poor boat handling	Practise depowering the sail and just gliding the boat without power in the rig. Just doing "s" turns into and out of the wind whilst staying on the foils is a good drill to improve boat handling.
Boat rears up as you turn	Poor boat set-up	The foils are not well balanced for gliding: try some more lift on the rudder.
Boat pitchpoles as you turn	Poor boat set-up	The foils are not well balanced for gliding: try less lift on the rudder or more angle of attack on the main foil.

Objective: To understand the adjustments that can be made to the foils.

Overview: As discussed previously, for the beginner, we would recommend a relatively low ride height to minimise crashes but, as you get more competent, you may want to start adjusting the foils.

ADJUSTING THE RIDE HEIGHT

The ride height may be adjusted in two ways: Firstly, you can lengthen or shorten the wand. Here you can see an adjustable wand, which allows the length to be adjusted by the sailor whilst sailing.

Secondly you can shorten or lengthen the push rod lengths. On many modern boats a ride height adjuster is available that allows this to be adjusted whilst sailing. By spinning the spindle, you can lengthen or shorten push rods. If you consider that 3 turns makes a significant difference to the ride height of the boat you need to handle this with care.

The different ways in which the ride height is adjusted will have an effect on how the boat sails. If you shorten the push rod length this has the effect of the wand working closer to the main foil and also affects the gearing of the control system.

By shortening or lengthening the wand you maintain the gearing and keep the wand working further forwards which gives less turbulence next to the foil and gives the flap further time to respond to waves. Many sailors use an adjustable wand and a ride height adjuster in tandem, others use just the ride height spindle, and others nothing at all: manually adjusting it before sailing.

Apart from adjusting the ride height the adjustment also accounts for the asymmetric nature of the wand mechanism (which is on one side of the boat): there is a significant height difference on each tack and, as you improve, this difference can be accounted for as you tack – that is if you do not have anything else to worry about!

The wand length being adjusted

Turning the push rod bottlescrew adjusts the push rod length

ADJUSTING THE ANGLE OF ATTACK

The angle of attack of a horizontal foil is critical to its performance. Often this is factory set and may or may not be adjustable. Most boats will have several pin positions and the F101 has a wheel and screw arrangement that allows infinite adjustment. If you consider that on the main foil we will have an effective working range that will vary over as little as 2-3 degrees you can see how critical this may be. Moths are looking at 0.5 degree increments as making substantial speed differences.

In general terms the angle of attack is always a set of compromises and its adjustment will rely on what parameters you are working against. For example, in lighter winds and with heavier loads you will need a higher angle of attack to get the boat in the air. The trade-off is that this will produce more drag so you won't ultimately go as fast. In stronger winds, when the boat speeds are higher, you can select a more efficient angle of attack as you will be generating the required amount of lift simply by going faster through the water.

The fundamentals of this are: the greater angle of attack, the more lift you generate ... but with more drag! On the main foil you can end up in a situation where the lift generated by the main foil is so great that the only way to keep the foil in the water is for the flap to try to send it back down, so you get them working against each other. Far better to reduce the angle of attack and then allow the flap to be more neutral in its action and this will work more efficiently and the boat will go faster as there is less drag. The angle of attack may also be adjusted by moving your bodyweight forwards or backwards OR by applying more or less lift to the rear of the boat as the rudder foil works in the same way: by rotating the tiller extension the angle of attack may be increased or decreased to add or subtract the amount of lift being generated at the back of the boat.

Winding up the tiller

Pin forward = more rudder lift (bow down)

Pin back = less rudder lift (bow up)

The table overleaf shows how you would adjust the basic set-up of your boat. This is for competent sailors; if you are learning, keep it nice and low and remember: weight forwards and / or more rudder lift immediately you start getting nervous / too high / out of control.

In lighter winds you will find that you will need to take off at an angle much closer to the wind so we have put the settings for early take off mode into the upwind section. It is easy to stall the foils out so don't put too much lift on initially with the angle of attack and rely on rolling backwards with your bodyweight only when you think you have reached take-off speed, get your weight forward again as soon as you are up out of the water.

The rule of thumb is using your most efficient settings as much as you can which means as little drag as possible. You move away from this rule in marginal foiling conditions (where you need more lift so can put up with a little more drag) or in overpowered conditions (when you need to decrease lift as the greater speeds are creating more than you need). Far more important is an understanding of what is going on with the foils that you cannot see purely by reacting to how the boat is behaving. This is learned over time and with experience but the benefit of having an outside observer who can feedback the issues and a remedy cannot be over

PART 3

emphasised. The rigging manual of your specific boat should be able to help with accurate settings.

What this table does not show is how you would tune the foils in differing water conditions. This is commonly known as 'gearing' and refers to the amount that the wand moves in relation to how much the flap on the main foil moves. This ratio can be adjusted in a number of ways on different boats including the length of the wand, the length of the various push rods and the length and angle of the cams and gears in the whole mechanism. This subject could fill a book in itself and is best catered for in the boat-specific manuals.

The fundamental basis of gearing is that the less

flap movement you have, the less drag you will have but arguably less control. If you have your flap moving a lot for every small movement your wand makes this will create a lot of drag on the foil and movement up and down of the boat (porpoising).

As a general rule:

- Lighter winds and flat water = less gearing
- Wavier water = more gearing

If only it were that simple! But, if you are at the stage that this is becoming something you want to investigate, then the Moth class have developed systems where you can adjust ALL of this whilst you are sailing.

ADJUSTMENTS TO THE BASIC SET-UP

	Angle of Attack	Ride Height	Rudder Lift	Body Position
MARGINAL FOILING CONDITIONS				
UPWIND	Medium / high	High	Medium	Middle / forwards
CROSS-WIND	High	High	Medium	Middle / back
DOWNWIND	High	High	Medium	Middle / back
CHAMPAGNE FOILING CONDITIONS				
UPWIND	Medium	High	Medium / high	Forwards
CROSS-WIND	Medium	High	Medium	Middle
DOWNWIND	Medium	Medium / high	Medium / high	Middle / forwards
FRESH TO FRUITY CONDITIONS				
UPWIND	Low to neutral	High	Medium	Middle
CROSS-WIND	Low to neutral	Medium / low	Medium / high	Middle / forwards
DOWNWIND	Low to neutral	Low	High	Forwards

Objective: To allow you to foil safely and to provide guidance for safety boat crew who might try to help you.

Overview: Safety, as in all watersports, is an aspect that should not be taken lightly. As a general rule the pre-requisite skills required for foiling have so far dictated a level of sailing experience that has kept reported incidents down to a low level. Dinghy foiling is so far proving to be as safe as other aspects of sailing but, as this side of the sport becomes more popular and easier to achieve, then it is certainly sensible to discuss ways in which you can keep yourself and others as safe as possible.

THE ABC OF FOILING SAFETY

Always foil in company.
This is really simple. Should something go wrong then you need someone to go and get help. Never sail alone (or without safety craft present).

Be aware of your limitations, your environment and other water users.
Know the limitations for your craft and its seaworthiness, your skill level and your level of fitness. It goes without saying that gear failure will ruin your day. Be aware that learning to foil can be very tiring when your skill level is low: get back to safety BEFORE you become exhausted.

Check the weather forecast and make sure that you know the local area in terms of tides as well as shallows, rocks and hazards. Foiling can be painful and expensive if you hit submerged objects. If in doubt, ASK the locals: remember not everywhere is suitable for foiling.

Always keep an eye on being able to get back to where you started: foilers can cover large distances pretty quickly and it is easy to lose sight of home.

Finally, consider other water users: stay away from swimming areas, and other craft. Foiling dinghies travel fast and closing speeds can be dangerous … and no-one likes a show off.

Check and wear your safety equipment
ALWAYS carry a knife on your person. In case you become entangled in lines or hiking straps, a knife in your buoyancy aid pocket will solve most issues.

Wearing a helmet, whilst a personal choice, should be considered and we would recommend it. Despite many viable arguments for not wearing one, we think it makes sense.

Buoyancy aids should be compulsory not only as flotation but also because they make great body armour too.

Appropriate levels of protection from sun, cold and wind should be worn, wetsuits help protect the body from abrasions and impacts and a good set of dinghy boots that protect your feet and ankles should be worn at all times. There is a lot of sail trimming involved so gloves are a good idea too.

SELF-HELP SAFETY TIPS

When learning, it is easier to go upwind than downwind where it can get become a bit too exciting for the beginner who has not yet mastered the required skills. To get downwind if things are becoming challenging you can try the following. I would suggest you practise these skills before you need to use them for real.

SAILING DOWNWIND BY STALLING THE MAINSAIL

The problems with sailing downwind generally revolve around the boat leaping out of the water due to the higher speeds and wave conditions that you can experience on this point of sailing. The trick here is to keep the boat low riding, bear away hard and fast and do not, in any circumstances, ease the mainsheet. If you can get the boat running down the edge of the no fly zone with the sail sheeted into the middle of the boat and the air flow effectively reversed on the sail then you can sail quite happily with the boat heeled over to windward balanced on the windward wing or float to a destination well downwind.

F101 sailing downwind with a stalled mainsail

Be careful, heading up to a point where too much sail is presented to the wind which will cause a capsize to leeward. Bearing away will cause a gybe and easing the sail may cause a leeward capsize or a pitchpole.

SAILING DOWNWIND BY DISCONNECTING THE WAND

If things have got simply too exciting to foil downwind you can also try disconnecting your wand to take off the lift from the main foil. This can be achieved by different means in different boats but releasing the pushrod from the foil in a Moth or Waszp and / or winding off the lift and / or the angle of attack by any means possible will have the same effect. No lift from the main foil and the boat will not fly.

This can have an unwanted effect however. The boat will have a tendency to nose dive with no main foil lift so make sure you put negative lift on the rudder by angling the foil away from the back of the boat and you still may have to hike off the back of the boat to prevent a nose dive.

Disconnecting the wand to sail safely downwind

BEING RESCUED BY A RIB

Foiling boats tend to be more fragile than the boats that your average safety boat driver will be used to dealing with so any contact with a RIB (avoid any solid safety boat contact if at all possible!) should be undertaken as a last resort.

We often use a RIB as a coach boat and, as foiling boats are becoming less rare in club environments, I thought it would be worth mentioning some nuggets that we have learned whilst using our RIBs around foiling boats.

I will break down how we deal with the boats in broad terms of capsized boats, coming alongside a righted boat and towing.

CAPSIZED BOAT

As I said, the boats are fragile and, if the boat is capsized, there are all sorts of obstructions ranging from rigs, hull, foils and, of course, sailors. Our golden rule is never to approach a capsized boat unless the sailor is trapped.

If the sailor needs to be extracted it is far better for them to swim cross-wind of the boat to the stern so that they do not go near to the delicate wand mechanism at the bow. They are also then in a position where the safety boat will not be in danger of drifting onto the capsized hull or foils nor of the boat flipping or drifting on to them as they turn off the engine to pull the sailor aboard.

Righting a capsized Moth can be fraught with difficulty. From the sailor's perspective, if the boat needs to be righted it is likely that they themselves are in the safety boat which at least gives the likelihood of there being a driver, a helper and a sailor. The sailor will have some knowledge of the boat, so this should help keep any potential damage down to a minimum.

The ideal scenario is that the Moth is conventionally capsized and the boat can be approached from downwind where the mast tip can be picked up from the bow and then slowly raised as the boat is driven up into the wind. Trying to recover the boat by pulling on the main foil should not be attempted: it can break, and it is expensive.

1 Approach the Moth from downwind

2 Pick up the mast tip

3 Slowly raise the mast

4 And drive the boat into the wind

5 So the boat comes upright alongside the RIB

6 And the wing can be held – opposite side to the throttle

- Don't be tempted to drive the RIB in to go for the main foil, ever.
- Only approach a capsized Moth from downwind of a beam reach and always go to the mast tip.
- Make sure the hull is upwind of the rig, otherwise wait … it should drift around or flip.

Don't be tempted to approach in a RIB if the rig is upwind and will not flip: I would always send the sailor back in to the water, if possible, to right the boat rather than risk an approach that can cause damage.

As you work your way up the rig, turn the boat into the wind and then just pop the bow through the wind (i.e. tack) so that the wing will be close to the RIB tube and the boom will be to leeward.

If at all possible, it is best to try to keep the wing on the opposite side to the throttle control of the RIB: this is a bonus as sometimes it just will not work out that way, but it is always worth being aware that having the wing over the RIB tube can nudge the throttle control if you are not conscious of it.

COMING ALONGSIDE A RIGHTED BOAT

Again, if possible, try to approach with the Moth the opposite side from the throttle. If you can't, be aware of the wing of the Moth and ensure that it is well clear of the controls.

- The sailor should set the windward wing in the air, standing, weight on centre of boat, front hand on wing, tiller extension and sheet in the back hand in a secure position.
- Beware, foils have horizontals so, if the boat capsizes further, you can cause damage on the underside of the RIB, but you also need to keep the windward wing high so the RIB can slip in underneath it.
- Ensure that the boat is not too close to the RIB particularly at the bow as the wand can easily be broken. Remember to take off the lift from the foils if you are going to tow!

You can go alongside the F101 with either of the wings in the water. If you are going to transfer crews then we prefer the windward wing in the water, but for the tow we would rest the windward float on top of the RIB tube.

1 Approach the Moth from astern to windward

2 The Moth should have its windward wing in the air

3 Slowly come alongside

4 And rest the wing on the RIB tube

TOWING

Whatever the foiling boat, before attempting any sort of tow, it is vital that you take off the lift from the foils. The sailor will know how to do this, but the safety boat crew may not. On Moths and the Waszp you will need to disconnect the wand control rod which attaches to the mechanism at the top of the main foil. This may be a pin and ring or a sprung clip.

The only way to 'tow' a Moth is with a side-by-side procedure. You can't rest a Moth, in a capsized position on the rig tube like you might a windsurfer, due to the standing rigging. You can get a Waszp to do this, as it has a freestanding rig, but we still prefer the conventional rig in the air, side-by-side approach. We never tow foiling boats using a line, it just does not work for a whole host of reasons.

To keep the boat attached to the side of the RIB it needs to be held by an 'extra' person who is sitting on the RIB tube in front of the forward beam. Just be aware that you can cause damage to the wing float underneath the trampoline if care is not taken.

The main issue with the side-by-side tow is that you will struggle to drive the safety boat at an angle much lower than a beam reach, driving faster can

bring the apparent wind forward but it has to be said that rescuing a Moth and taking it downwind is VERY difficult.

Depending on how far you have to go, the other options might be backing down (very short distances only!) or, if you have a long way to go, then you may have little option than to de-rig the boat which is difficult and likely to cause damage.

Taking the boat upwind should not cause any major difficulties aside thinking ahead if you may need to tack the boat to get to your final destination.

With the Waszp you can disconnect the mainsheet and, because the boat has no standing rigging, the sail can be allowed to swing freely in front of the mast, if required, allowing you to tow in any direction required.

The F101 has the advantage of having a lot of volume AND the ability to drop sails so you can pretty much treat it like a conventional boat in terms of rescue if you can deal with the foils not lifting, so either raise the foils and secure them in this position, get rid of the lift off the main foil and put negative lift on the rudder (see p46) or ensure you go at speeds below 6 knots.

Waszp being towed alongside a RIB

As outlined earlier (p20), most boats can foil if pushed through the water at the right angle and with enough speed. It is therefore inevitable that some existing dinghies are being converted to offer foiling.

The leading company in this market are Glide Free Design, formed in Australia by Ian Ward (who created the first in-line foiling Moth – see p17) and Peter Stephinson. They currently supply a number of conversion kits including for the Laser, RS Aero, Open Bic and D-Zero.

Some sailing organisations, training centres and holiday companies are using such converted boats not only to give people a foiling experience, but also to teach people to foil. How suitable these are for this purpose compared to craft designed for foiling will become clearer over time, but it is likely that the more modern, lighter boats stand the best chance, although even they are unlikely to give the opportunity to do a foiling tack.

Private individuals considering this route are advised to check what they are likely to be able to achieve in their chosen craft – whether they will just foil in a straight line or be able to successfully achieve a foiling gybe and / or tack. It would also be worth checking whether fitting these kits has any implications on the warranty of the original craft.

Conversion kits available from Glide Free Design

GLOSSARY

Aerofoil: A shape used to create lift, which could be, for example, an aeroplane wing, a sail, the vertical foils in a conventional dinghy or the horizontal foils on a foiling boat. Also known as airfoil.

Apparent wind: The wind experienced by a moving object, made up of the true wind and the wind created by the object's movement.

Batten: Strip inserted horizontally into the sail to help hold its shape.

Beating: Sailing as close to the wind as possible (also close-hauled and upwind).

Beam reach: Sailing at 90 degrees to the wind.

Bear(ing) away: Turning the boat away from the wind.

Block-to-block: Mainsail sheeted in completely so that the blocks are touching each other.

Boom: Horizontal spar attached to the mast that supports the mainsail.

Bow: Front of the boat.

Bridle: A loop made out of rope.

Broad reach: Sailing away from the wind at an angle of about 120 degrees from the wind.

Bulkhead: Front end of the cockpit or internal structures to ensure the rigidity of the hull.

Chine: Line of crease in the hull.

Clew: Corner of the sail away from the mast or forestay.

Close-hauled: Sailing as close to the wind as possible (also beating).

Close reach: Sailing at around 60 degrees to the wind.

Code zero: Asymmetric fore-sail sail like a gennaker.

Cross-shore wind: Wind blowing parallel to the beach.

Cunningham: A control line to tighten the luff of a sail (also downhaul).

Daggerboard: Vertical foil near the centre of the boat to prevent leeway (sideways slip).

De-power: Reduce the power in the rig.

Drag: One component of aerodynamic force which acts to reduce speed.

Downhaul: A control line to tighten the luff of a sail (also cunningham).

Downwind: Sailing away from the wind (also running).

Ease: To let out a sheet controlling a sail.

Falls of mainsheet: The lengths of mainsheet that fall between between the mainsheet blocks on the boom and the bridle.

Foil: Strictly any item with an aerofoil shape, but mainly used in this book to describe the horizontal foils that provide lift that are attached to the daggerboard and rudder (which are also foils!).

Foil pin: Pin to control the angle of attack of the foils.

Foot: The bottom edge of the sail.

Forestay: Wire that supports the mast at the bow of the boat.

Furl: Roll up a sail.

Goal point: Point selected to steer towards.

Gunwale: Outer edge of the side of a boat.

Gybe / gybing: Steering the boat from one side of the wind to the other when sailing downwind.

Gybing angle: The angle between downwind on port tack and downwind on starboard tack.

Halyard: Line used to hoist sails up the mast.

Head to wind: The boat pointing directly into the wind.

Hiking strap: Webbing straps which sailors can put their feet under to lean out (also toestraps).

Kicking strap: Control system to hold the boom

down and control the shape of the mainsail by pulling down on the leach of the sail (also vang).

King post: Post the mast is stepped in.

Leech: Back edge of a sail.

Leg-over: Method of righting and getting into a capsized boat.

Leeward: Away from the wind.

Lift: One component of aerodynamic force which acts to create lift.

Loos gauge: Device to measure the tension in wire rigging.

Low riding: Sailing a foiling boat in displacement mode (not on the foils).

Luff: Leading edge of a sail.

Luff: To turn the boat closer to the wind.

Mach 2: Design of an International Moth.

Mainsail: Sail on the boat attached to the back edge of the mast.

Mainsheet: Control line to adjust the trim of the mainsail.

Mainsheet falls: The lengths of mainsheet that fall between between the mainsheet blocks on the boom and the bridle.

Mast: Vertical spar that holds the sails in position.

Mast pin: Pin on the base of the mast which allows the mast to rotate on the king post of a Moth.

Mast tip: Top of the mast.

Mast rake: Fore and aft angle of the mast from vertical.

May stick: The extension at the top of the wand that allows it to be pulled backwards and downwards by elastic to keep the wand in contact with the water surface, named after UK Moth sailor, Adam May.

Neutral lift: The point at which the foils produce the amount of lift to maintain the boat's altitude at a constant height.

Offshore wind: Wind blowing off the land away from the beach.

Onshore wind: Wind blowing onto the land / beach.

Outhaul: Control line to adjust the position of the clew of the sail on the boom.

Pitchpole: Capsizing forwards end over end.

Push rod: A stainless steel control rod that is found between linkages making up the ride height control system

Reach / Reaching: Sailing roughly at right angles to the wind.

Ride height: Height the boat flies above the water surface.

Rig tension: Tension created in the rig by adjusting the shrouds and forestay.

Rudder: Vertical foil which is turned to steer the boat.

Running: Sailing away from the wind (also downwind).

Sailing position: The posture taken up by the sailor to allow dynamic body movement changes whilst enabling rapid sheet trimming and fine adjustments to steering.

Secure position: The posture taken up by the sailor where the boat is balanced and unlikely to capsize and the body is in a dynamic position where it can move quickly to stabilise the boat and prevent a capsize.

Sheet: Rope used to control a sail.

Sheeting in / out: Pulling a sail's sheet in or easing it (also trimming).

Shroud: Wires either side of the mast which hold the mast in place.

Shroud plate: Device to attach the shroud to the hull.

Slip knot: Temporary knot which can easily be released.

Spreader / prodder bracket: Metal rods (and its attachment point) that stick out from the mast and connect to the shrouds to support the mid-section of the mast.

Stern: Back of the boat.

Tack / tacking: Steering the boat through the wind.

Tacking angle: The angle between close-hauled on port tack and close-hauled on starboard tack.

Telltale: Lightweight thread or sailcloth attached to the sail or shrouds to show the wind's movement.

Tiller: Carbon or aluminium tube attached to the rudder which enables steering.

Tiller extension: A carbon or aluminium tube connected to the tiller which the helmsman holds to control the tiller and thereby the rudder which enables the boat to be steered.

Toestraps: Webbing straps which sailors can put their feet under to lean out (also hiking straps).

Trailing edge: Back edge of a foil.

Trampoline: Webbing platform between the hull and wing bars.

Tramp(oline) **lacing:** Lacing to hold the trampoline tightly in place.

Transom: Furthest back part of the hull.

Trim / trimming: Pulling a sail's sheet in or easing it (also sheeting in / out).

Trolley: Device on which the boat is supported and moved around on whilst ashore.

True wind: The wind direction experienced when stationary.

Upwind: Sailing as close to the wind as possible (also beating and close-hauled).

Vang: Control system to hold the boom down and control the shape of the mainsail by pulling down on the leach of the sail (also kicking strap).

Vent / venting: Letting air in or out of the hull to get to the same pressure as outside the hull to prevent water ingress.

Wand: Stick attached to the bow or bowsprit which measures and controls the height of the hull from the water surface.

Wand preventer: Line which prevents the wand from being pushed forwards if the boat should move backwards.

Water start: Method of entering a boat from in the water.

Wind blind: State of not knowing where the wind is coming from.

Windward: Towards the wind.

Wing: Part of a foiling dinghy sticking out from the hull consisting of a trampoline and wing bar that increases the righting moment of the boat.

Wing bar: Edge of the wing to which the trampoline is attached.

Wing float: Degree of flotation provided at the edge of the wing.

Wipe-out: Capsize.

ACKNOWLEDGEMENTS

A great many people have helped in the production of this book and the author and publisher would like to thank them all. These include:

PHOTOGRAPHS
Domenico Bofti
Matthew Botfield
Brett Burvill
Dave Clark
Walter Cooper
Geoff Cox
Paloma Bermejo Cuevas
Chris Eades
Clive Everest
Foiling Week
James Grogono
Tom Gruitt
Alan Hillman
David Hillman
Tim Hore
John Ilett
Richard Langdon
Sam Le Lievre
Kiko Martinez
Simon Morgan
Peter Muller
Gerald New
Martina Orsini
Andy Patterson
Ian Ward

FOILING HISTORY & DEVELOPMENT
Ken Baker
Brett Burvill
Dave Clark
Clive Everest
James Grogono
John Ilett
Mike Lennon
Adam May
Andy Patterson
Ian Ward